IN PRINT

Beginning Literacy Through Cultural Awareness

Lynellyn D. Long
Janet Spiegel-Podnecky

▼▼ Addison-Wesley Publishing Company

Reading, Massachusetts • Menlo Park, California • New York
Don Mills, Ontario • Wokingham, England • Amsterdam • Bonn
Sydney • Singapore • Tokyo • Madrid • Bogota • Santiago • San Juan

Acknowledgments

We gratefully acknowledge our friends—coworkers and students—at the Jamaica Plain Adult Learning Program and the International Institute of Boston for their help in writing this book. We would also like to thank the United Nations Volunteers (UNVs) in the Philippines Refugee Processing Center (1980–81), the Hmong and Lao refugees in Ban Vinai, and the Refugee Women's Program in San Francisco for what they have taught us about literacy. In particular, we must thank the following individuals for their direct contributions to this work: Ellen Basu, Teresa A. Brown, John Croes, Shirley Brice Heath, Rebecca Hovey, Judith Langer, Moira Lucey, Lotte and Alan Marcus, Jennifer Nourse, Joan Penning, Mary Ann Perry, Carey Reid, Michelle Roszko, Dee Horne Thompson, Dianne Walker, and David Ziemba. Finally, this entirely joint production of ours would not have been possible without the love and support of Josef Podnecky and Dennis Long.

A publication of the World Language Division

Sponsoring Editor: Kathy Sands-Boehmer
Developmental Editor: Jennifer Bixby
Manufacturing/Production: James W. Gibbons
Illustrations: Jamie Treat
Design: Baskerville Book and Editorial Services Company
Photograph research: Merle Sciacca
Cover design: Gary Fujiwara

Manuscript Reviewers: Lisa Bassett, Evanston Township High School/Adult Education Program; Cindy Greenberg, Queens College/CUNY; and Vicky Money, El Paso Community College

Photographs: p. 1, Brown Leonard; p. 16, Carey Reid, Jamaica Plain Adult Learning Program; p. 25, Elihu Blotnick; p. 36, Metropolitan Transportation Authority, New York City; p. 46, Elizabeth Sweeney; p. 58, Lawrence Memorial Hospital of Medford; p. 72, Boston Housing Authority; p. 84, Arthur Lavine, The Chase Manhattan Bank; p. 96, American Red Cross; p. 109, Elihu Blotnick; p. 121, Lynellyn D. Long; p. 133, Rafael Millan; p. 148, Northern Essex Community College; p. 159, Josef Podnecky; p. 169, Mark Morelli.

Credits: p. 140, Registry of Vital Records and Statistics, Mass. Dept. of Public Health; p. 175, copyright, NYNEX Information Resources Company, 1984. Printed by permission of NYNEX Information Resources Company.

DEFGHIJ-AL-943210
ISBN: 0-201-12023-2

Contents

Introduction

We address the following remarks to the adult learners who will use this book and to their family, friends, and teachers, who teach and assist them. Teachers and administrators should also read the *Teacher's Guide*.

Who?

We wrote *In Print* for adults learning to read and write English. Each chapter is organized around a theme of interest to adult immigrants as well as native English speakers. We found that adults in general are used to learning by doing, so we start with writing from the beginning, reversing the usual reading to writing order used in teaching children. *In Print* makes learning literacy an active process for adult learners.

Many of our learners were immigrants in ESL classes, but some were native English speakers. Because the topics and activities relate to adult daily life and concerns, *In Print* is appropriate for native English speakers. Adults who are not literate in their first language have also used these lessons successfully. However, we recommend learners become literate first in their native tongue. This will help in becoming literate in English.

People often ask us when to begin these lessons. We usually begin after two or three months of beginning ESL. Many adults associate studying with reading and writing and demand literacy in their language classes so it helps to begin early on. Learners also observed that it was easier to learn English once they could write it down and see it.

What?

This book helps learners to become literate in three ways. First, it helps in every day reading and writing tasks. Learners become more self-sufficient when they can read their own bills or complete their children's school forms. Illiteracy is stigmatized no matter how intelligent the person is. Being able to do some of the simpler reading and writing tasks can make a difference with jobs, educational opportunities, services, and self-esteem.

Second, this book helps learners in recording their stories and experiences. Many immigrants want their children and grandchildren to remember their cultural roots and traditions. They also want other Americans to hear their point of view. This book exposes learners to many different forms of literate expression; from documenting personal experiences to complaining about inflation.

Finally, this book helps learners use literacy to increase their understanding of American society and ways of doing things. Much of American life is organized with the assumption that the person is literate in English. Time schedules, computer programs, application forms, bills, and jobs assume literacy. Literacy can change the way we organize knowledge, remember past events, or tell a story. Consequently, becoming literate provides a deeper understanding of the language and culture of this society.

How?

We organized each chapter around themes which reflect the lives and experiences of our adult learners. Each group of learners has a unique set of experiences to share. Thus, teachers and friends should feel free to adapt the lessons to fit the learners' particular situations.

Each chapter opens with a photograph and question that serve as a starting point for discussion. After talking about the photograph, begin with *Talk*. Here you can discuss the main themes of the chapter and review useful vocabulary, spending about half of the first session for each new chapter on *Talk*. Start with the Discussion Questions and then continue with More Questions on subsequent days. You can make the *Talk* section a part of each lesson. Select the questions that seem most appropriate to the learners. Native English speakers can discuss the questions in terms of their own backgrounds. It is not necessary to do all of the questions. Conclude with Summary Questions in the last lesson on the chapter.

Write and Read follows *Talk*. If you are helping the learner, work together to fill in the chart. Explain the coordinates and together illustrate the learner's ideas with drawings, photographs, and words. Practice by redoing the chart in the book or in a separate notebook. The learner finishes by reading the results aloud.

In the *Look* section, the learner gains new sight word skills. Read the sight words aloud together. The learner then practices finding the sight words in the text and circles them. The texts get progressively more difficult from a few words and puzzles to full-length articles.

In the *Listen* section, the learner works on phonics skills. In the beginning chapters, the teacher or helper pronounces one of the sounds for the learner to circle. Use the hard "g" and "c" sounds in these lessons and consult the Teacher's Guide to pronounce the sounds correctly. In later lessons, help learners form sounds into words and sound out the new words. The *Analyze* section focuses on structural analysis skills. In these exercises, show the learner how to put syllables, prefixes, and suffixes together to form words. Then, help the learner to sound out the new words.

The *Do* activities give learners a chance to apply their new literacy skills to some everyday tasks. If you are helping the learner, first discuss how the form or application is used. Often the learner has come across these forms before, so discuss what information is needed. Together read the material and then assist the learner in completing it. When the form or application is completed, the learner should read back the results.

In the *Explain* section, the learner demonstrates reading comprehension. These exercises require the learner to match words and concepts, put words in context, fill in blanks, or put sentences in sequential order. If you are helping the learner, show what is required and correct the answers together. Review material that was difficult.

In the final section, *Write and Read Again*, learners and helpers should review the material orally together. Then show the learner how to write one of the sentences or stories. The learner can write other sentences, and later stories, using the examples provided or make up his/her own on the same themes. The learner may also want to keep a journal or notebook of these writings to show progress over time and to develop different written forms.

How long?

It doesn't matter how long people take. Some finish the book in six months, others take more than a year. Learners and their teachers should not get discouraged. Learning to read and write (or teaching someone else to) can be enjoyable and rewarding. This book provides some tools. Those who practice often in the course of their normal activities will progress more quickly. Encourage learners to read and write outside of class: bus billboards, street signs, notes to friends. Making reading and writing part of everyday life makes a literate person.

Why?

Why this book? We wrote *In Print* originally for our own classes because we wanted materials that:

- respected the intelligence and experiences of adult learners;
- were relevant to the lives of immigrants and people who must struggle to get a better education; and
- encouraged learners to create their own English literacies—ones that expressed their realities and concerns.

This book is written with the hope that those who use it will someday write their own.

It's in Print

When do you need to read or write English?

 # Talk

literacy

read

write

DISCUSSION

Can you read or write _____ ?
Are you learning to read and write _____ ?
Why do you want to read and write English?

MORE QUESTIONS

Who reads and writes in your family?
Who can help you read and write English?
What can you read on the street?
What can you read and write at home?
What can you read and write at work?
What can you read on TV?
How long will it take you to learn to read and write English?
What do you want to read or write in English?
When do you need to read or write English?
What can you learn in a literacy class?

SUMMARY

How can you learn to read and write English?

Write and Read

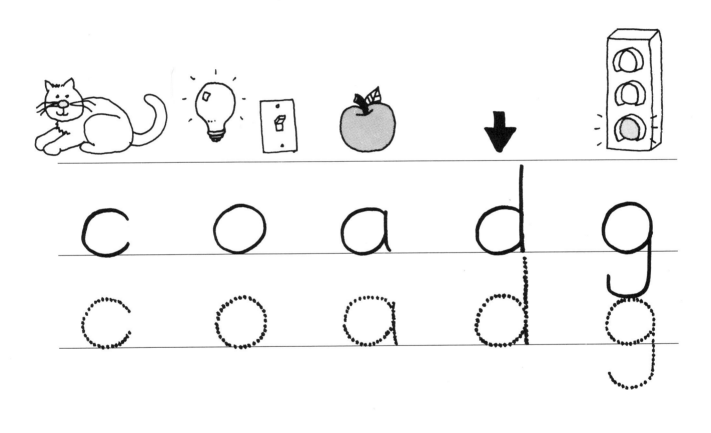

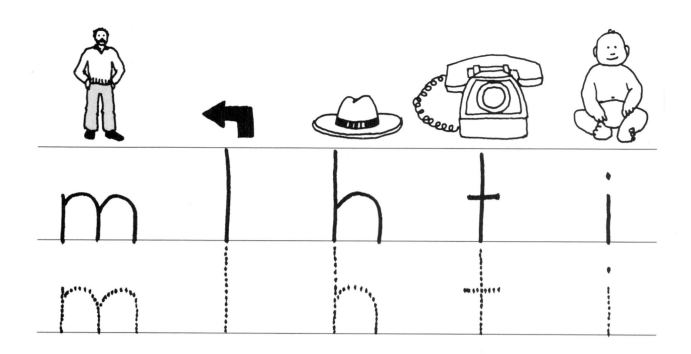

m   l   h   t   i

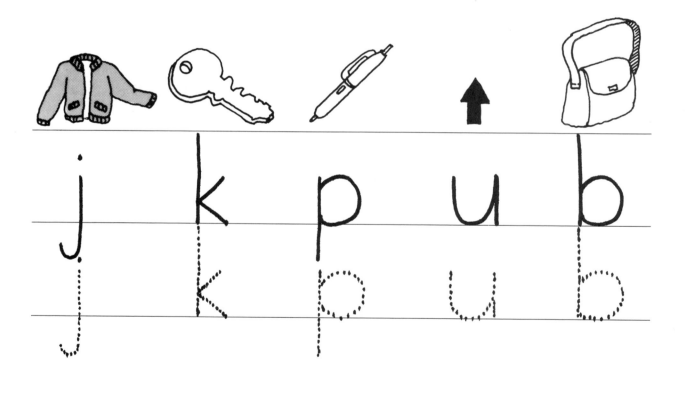

j   k   p   u   b

r f n e s

r f n e s

w y v x z q

w y v x z q

5

0   1   2   3   4

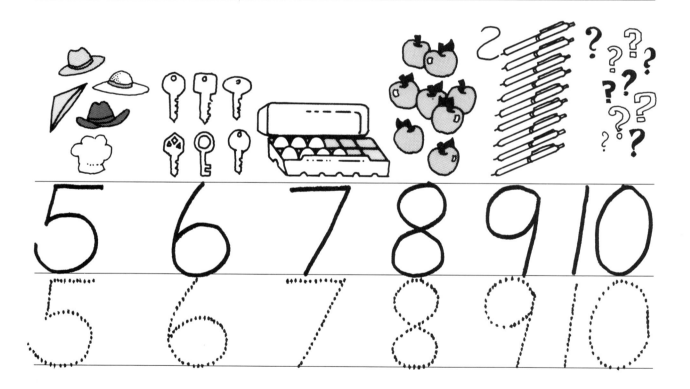

5   6   7   8   9   10

 Listen

1. p   (g)   h

2. c   m   l

3. t   b   u

4. d   w   n

5. r   s   e

6. f   c   b

7. a   o   h

8. t   i   s

9. m   d   o

10. b   a   r

1.	652	779	(982)
2.	125	860	943
3.	821	653	459
4.	451	415	455
5.	698	689	968
6.	253	359	285
7.	703	307	370
8.	921	129	902
9.	348	384	584
10.	622	262	206

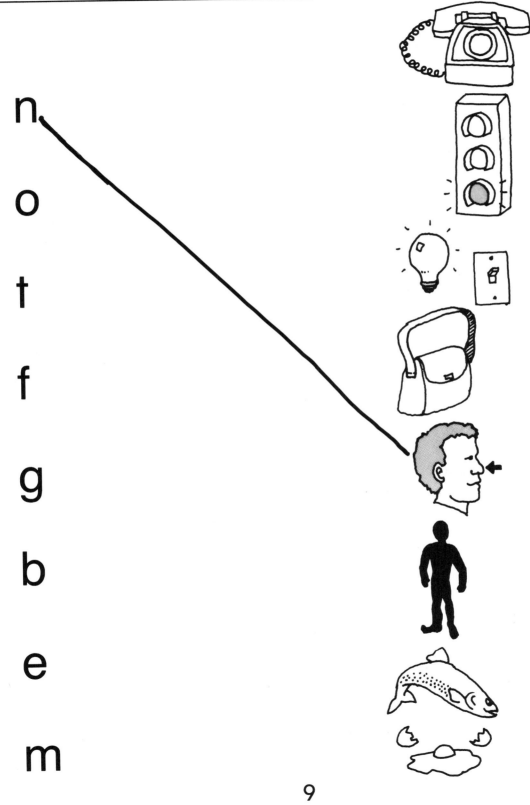

n

o

t

f

g

b

e

m

9

A.

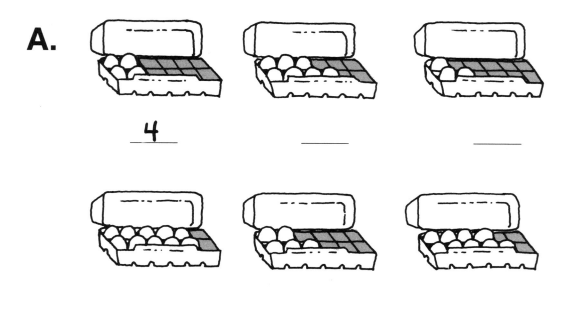

4 ___   ___   ___

___   ___   ___

B.   **u**   **d**   **r**   **l**

u   ___   ___   ___

___   ___   ___   ___

Aa Bb Cc Dd Ee Ff Gg Hh Ii
Jj Kk Ll Mm Nn Oo Pp Qq Rr
Ss Tt Uu Vv Ww Xx Yy Zz

A	b	ⓐ	c
M	m	n	s
R	l	f	r
T	t	e	h
D	s	t	d
G	i	p	g
E	b	e	w

n	U	M	N
w	X	H	W
p	P	B	G
f	K	F	R
h	M	E	H
i	I	L	T
r	E	R	P
b	B	D	Z
l	Y	J	L
s	C	S	E

 Do

S STOP

N 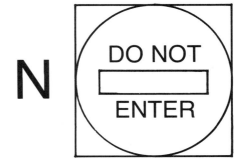 DO NOT ENTER

W DONT WALK

R FOR RENT / RESTAURANT

A AVE.

P OPEN

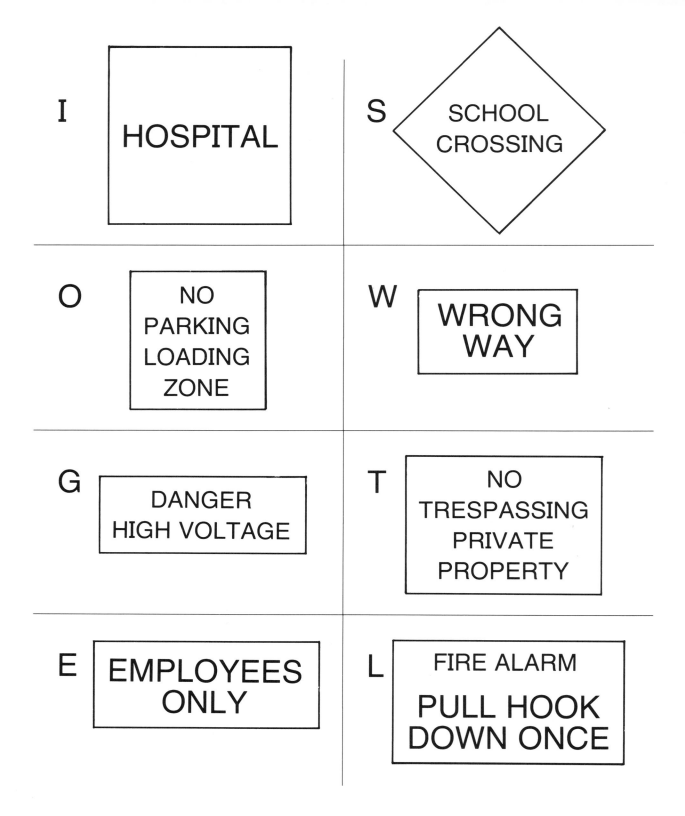

I HOSPITAL

S SCHOOL CROSSING

O NO PARKING LOADING ZONE

W WRONG WAY

G DANGER HIGH VOLTAGE

T NO TRESPASSING PRIVATE PROPERTY

E EMPLOYEES ONLY

L FIRE ALARM PULL HOOK DOWN ONCE

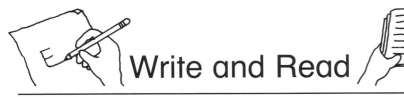 
C c	O _	A _	D _
G _	M _	L _	H _
T _	I _	J _	K _
P _	U _	B _	R _
F _	N _	E _	S _
W _	Y _	V _	X _

2
Changing Roles

Who goes to school?

 Talk

```
┌─────────────────┐
│                 │
│      men        │
│                 │
│     women       │
│                 │
└─────────────────┘
```

DISCUSSION

What do women do every day in _____ ?
(in your country)

What do women do every day in the U.S.?

What do men do every day in _____ ?

What do men do every day in the U.S.?

MORE QUESTIONS

Who took care of your family in _____ ?

Who buys the food in your family?

Who makes the money?

Who pays the bills?

Who takes care of the children?

Who cooks the food?

Who cleans the house?

Who goes to work?

Who goes to school?

SUMMARY

What can men do now in the U.S.?

What can women do now in the U.S.?

Write and Read

	MEN	WOMEN
LAOS		
USA		

 Listen

A.

1.	am	at
2.	an	at
3.	am	an
4.	it	in
5.	im	it
6.	in	im
7.	at	it
8.	im	am

B.

1.	in	it	im
2.	at	an	am
3.	am	in	it
4.	im	it	an
5.	an	in	it
6.	it	an	at
7.	im	am	an
8.	at	it	am

 Explain

A.

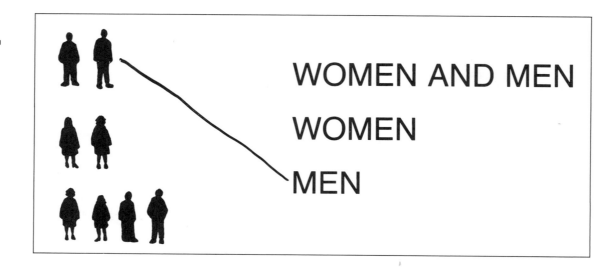

WOMEN AND MEN

WOMEN

MEN

B.

| WOMEN | MEN |

 Look

1. MEN   ME   MEN

2. WOMEN   WOMEN   WOME

3. NAEM   NAME   NAME

4. DATE   DATE   DAET

5. NAME   MANE   NAME

6. DETA   DATE   DATE

7. ADDRESS   ADDRESS   ADDESS

8. TELEPHONE   TELEPLONE   TELEPHONE

 Do

NAME _____

ADDRESS _____

_____

TELEPHONE _____

DATE _____ ___ M

___ F

NAME _____ ☐ M

TELEPHONE _____ ☐ F

ADDRESS _____

_____

DATE _____

NAME _____ ___ M

ADDRESS _____ ___ F

_____

TELEPHONE _____

DATE _____

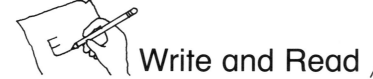 

1. Are you at 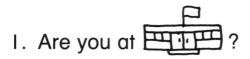 ?   Yes, I am at  .

2. Are you at 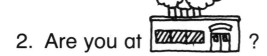 ?   Yes, I am at  .

3. Are you at 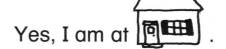 ?   Yes, I am at 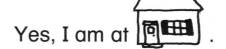 .

4. Are you at the 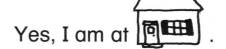 ?   Yes, I am at the 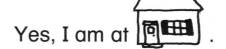 .

5. Are you at the 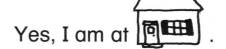 ?   Yes, I am at the 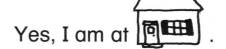 .

6. Are you from   Yes, I am from

_____ ?   _____ .

24

3
Children of Two Cultures

What do children do after school?

 Talk

children

school

home

DISCUSSION

How many children are in your family?
How old are your children?
Where were your children born?

MORE QUESTIONS

How many children do you have?
Do your children go to school?
Where do your children go to school?
How old are school children?
Who takes care of children when parents work?
Do you take care of children?
Do children take care of children?
What do children do after school?
How old were your children when they came to the U.S.?
What language do your children speak at home?   At school?
What do you do if the children have a problem?

SUMMARY

What do you want your children to do in the U.S.?
How can you help your children?

Write and Read

The Dostali Family

Al

Martha

Rosa   Linda   David

Parents

    Al

    Linda

Children

    Martha

    David

    Rosa

The _____ Family

Parents

_____

_____

Children

_____

_____

_____

_____

 Listen

A.

1.	in	ig
2.	im	id
3.	ag	am
4.	ad	an
5.	am	ag
6.	at	ot
7.	im	am
8.	ig	og

B.

1.	in	on	an
2.	am	im	om
3.	it	at	ot
4.	od	id	ad
5.	ig	og	ag
6.	at	ot	it
7.	on	in	an
8.	am	om	im

SCHOOL

Dostali

LAST NAME

AGE

David

FIRST NAME

5 years old

CHILD CARE

CHILDREN

 **Explain**

CHILDREN	FIRST NAME
SCHOOL	CHILD CARE
AGE	LAST NAME

 David

_____   _____   _____

 5 years old   Dostali

_____   _____   _____

 Look

1. AGE   AGE   AG

2. SCHOO   SCHOOL   SCHOOL

3. CHILDREN   CHILDREN   CHILDRE

4. DATE   DTAE   DATE

5. FIRST   FRIST   FIRST

6. ACE   AGE   AGE

7. SCOOL   SCHOOL   SCHOOL

8. LAST   LOST   LAST

31

```
A   S   N   A   M   E   L
D   C   E   G   O   W   A
I   H  (M   E   N)  A   S
W   O   M   E   N   U   T
N   O   A   D   A   T   E
E   L   F   I   R   S   T
```

MEN ✓

WOMEN

DATE

AGE

NAME

FIRST

LAST

SCHOOL

 # Do

SCHOOL INFORMATION FORM

PARENTS

NAME _____ AGE _____
              LAST   FIRST

NAME _____ AGE _____
              LAST   FIRST

CHILDREN

	FIRST NAME	AGE	DATE OF BIRTH	NAME OF SCHOOL
1				
2				
3				
4				
5				
6				

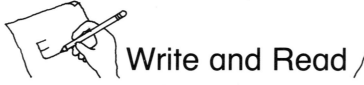 
In the Cruz family,

there are two
children.

In my family,

there _____
_____.

In the Vilay family,

the parents work.

In my family,

the _____
_____.

34

In the Jackson family,

the children take care
of children.

In my family,

the _____
of children.

In the Lee family,

the woman goes to
school.

In my family,

_____
_____.

In the DeSantos
family,

the children go to day
care.

In my family,

_____
_____.

4
Working from Experience

What time do you go to work?

 **Talk**

```
┌─────────────────────┐
│      work           │
│                     │
│   experience        │
└─────────────────────┘
```

DISCUSSION

What was your job in _____ ?

What job(s) can you do now?

Are you working now?

MORE QUESTIONS

What time did you go to work in _____ ?

What time do you go to work in the U.S.?

Who was your supervisor in _____ ?

Who is your supervisor now?

How much money did workers make in _____ ?

How much money do workers make here?

How many people work in your family?

Who works in your family?

SUMMARY

What jobs can you do?

What job do you want to have 20 years from now?

Before   Now

Honduras	Denver
$3.00/hr.	$4.00/hr.
7:00 am - 6:00 pm	7:00 am - 3:00 pm

 Listen

1. ⓜ ap ⓐⓝ ad		man
2. h op og ot		_____
3. c at ash ap		_____
4. r ob on ot		_____
5. f it ish in		_____
6. j ob ot on		_____
7. d ip id ish		_____
8. c an at ab		_____

39

A.

1.	sit	hit	pit
2.	not	lot	hot
3.	fan	pan	can
4.	rob	job	lob
5.	wish	fish	dish

B.

1.	sag	sam	sat
2.	can	cad	cab
3.	hot	hog	hop
4.	fat	fan	fab
5.	chin	chip	chit

C.

1.	hat	hot	hit
2.	did	dad	dod
3.	rap	rop	rip
4.	big	bag	bog
5.	mad	mid	mod

 Explain

1. She is a   2. _____   3. _____

_____

4. _____   5. _____   6. _____

_____

farmer   painter   teacher
bus driver   cook   janitor

 Explain

PHONE	April 7, 1986
JOB	012-58-6280
DATE	130 Western Ave. Denver, CO 80205
SOC. SEC.	32 years old
AGE	356-8904
DATES	farmer
ADDRESS	1975–1982
NAME	Elena Vargas

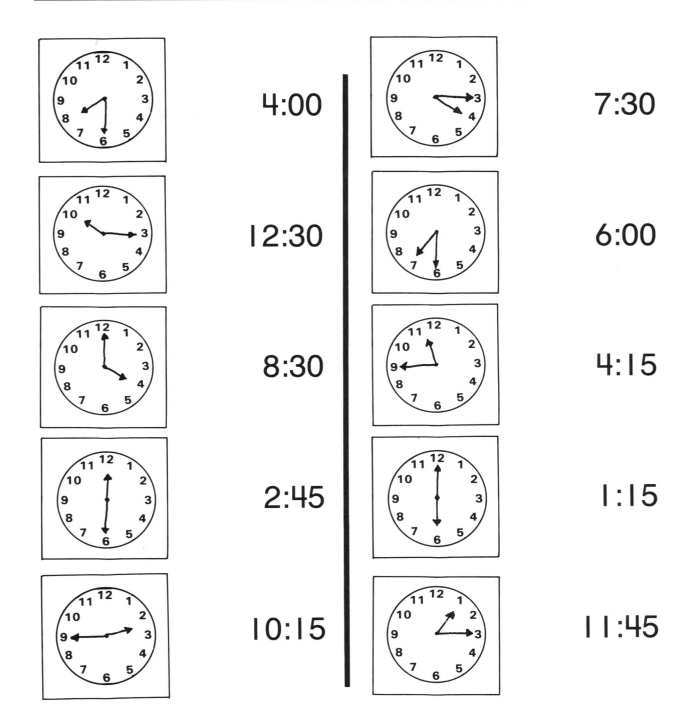

4:00

7:30

12:30

6:00

8:30

4:15

2:45

1:15

10:15

11:45

43

 Do

---

APPLICATION FOR WORK

NAME _____ DATE _____

           LAST   FIRST

PHONE # _____ SOC. SEC. # _____

ADDRESS _____

_____

JOB DESIRED _____

WORK EXPERIENCE

	JOB	ADDRESS	DATES
1			
2			
3			

 **Write and Read**  **Again**

1. He was a fisherman from 1962 to 1973 in Vietnam.

What? _____
When? _____
Where? _____

2. She was a cook from 1976 to 1982 in Ethiopia.

What? _____
When? _____
Where? _____

3. She was a salesperson from 1980 to 1983 in Laos.

What? _____
When? _____
Where? _____

4. I was a _____
_____
_____ .

What? _____
When? _____
Where? _____

45

5
Other Tongues, Other Worlds

Where do Americans come from?

 **Talk**

---

language
country

DISCUSSION

Where is your country?
What languages do you speak?

MORE QUESTIONS

Who taught you _____ ?
When did you learn to speak _____ ?
Can you read and write _____ ?
How old were you when you learned to read and write?
When do you speak _____ in the U.S.?
When do you speak English?
Who can translate for you?
When do you speak to other Americans?
Where do other Americans come from?
Do all Americans speak English?
What languages do Americans speak?

SUMMARY

Why are many languages spoken in the U.S.?

	Where? **What language?** **When?**	**Where?** **What language?** **When?**
Marcia Sabares 	Bogotá, Colombia Spanish From 1962 to 1983	New York, USA English From 1983 to ____
(You)		

 Listen

1. m	et	en	ed	_____
2. r	un	ub	um	_____
3. p	eg	ep	en	_____
4. b	un	ug	em	_____
5. t	en	et	ed	_____
6. sh	ug	ut	un	_____
7. s	um	ub	un	_____
8. b	et	ed	en	_____

A.

1.	pen	when	men
2.	met	let	wet
3.	rug	mug	bug
4.	cut	but	nut
5.	fed	red	bed

B.

1.	bug	bum	bud
2.	men	met	meg
3.	shug	shun	shut
4.	peg	pet	pen
5.	hum	hug	hut

C.

1.	ten	tan	tin
2.	bog	big	beg
3.	cop	cap	cup
4.	pin	pen	pun
5.	chop	chip	chap

 Analyze

tel	ad	fam
dish	chil	jan
num	fish	

43 Central Ave.
Bayside, NY 01499

_____ dress

 _____ itor

2
4   5
17   9
3   24

_____ bers

 _____ erman

 _____ ephone

 _____ ily

 _____ washer

51

 **Explain**

Be quiet.   Good-bye.

Hello.   Don't smoke.

Nice to meet you.

_____   _____   _____

_____   _____

Hasta luego.

 Look

N A T I O N A L I T Y E

D D E N A M E A G E T D

A D X E M S P N O P W O

T R P D F O L G S U O C

E E E N I C O U N T R Y

O S R A R S M A B A K T

F S I H S E A G O T E W

E C E B T C L E L A S T

N A N E O A D M O P I U

T R C U S T I E G K O S

R T E L E P H O N E N T

Y D A T E O F B I R T H

NAME	NATIONALITY	DATE OF BIRTH
AGE	LANGUAGE	DATE OF ENTRY
ADDRESS	COUNTRY	LAST
TELEPHONE	SOC. SEC.	FIRST
WORK	EXPERIENCE	

54

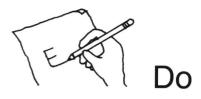 Do

PERSONAL INFORMATION

Please Print

NAME _____

            LAST   FIRST

                             M ☐

SOC.SEC. NO. _____ F ☐

AGE _____ DATE OF BIRTH _____

TELEPHONE NO. _____

ADDRESS _____

_____

U.S. CITIZEN?   ☐ YES

                     ☐ NO

NATIONALITY _____

DATE OF ENTRY _____

ALIEN REGISTRATION NO. _____

          SIGNATURE _____

          DATE _____

Signs in the United States

1.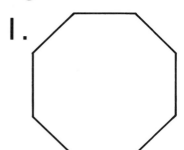
2.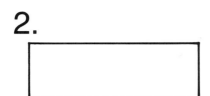
3.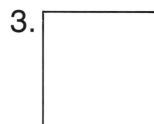

International Signs

4.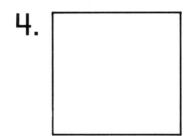
5.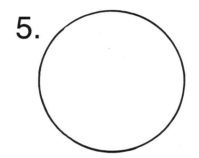
6.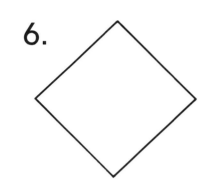

Signs in My Native Country

7.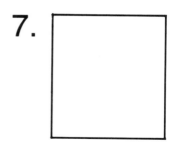
8.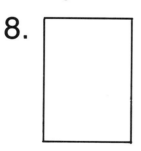
9.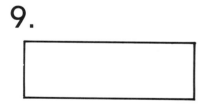

Pierre's Story

Pierre comes from Haiti. He lives in Charleston.

He speaks Creole.

Pierre can read and write French.

He can speak English.

He cannot read English.

But, his son can help him.

My Story

I come from _____ . I live in _____ .

I speak _____ .

I can (not) read _____ .

I can speak _____ .

I can _____ English.

But, _____ .

57

6
Cold Days and Runny Noses

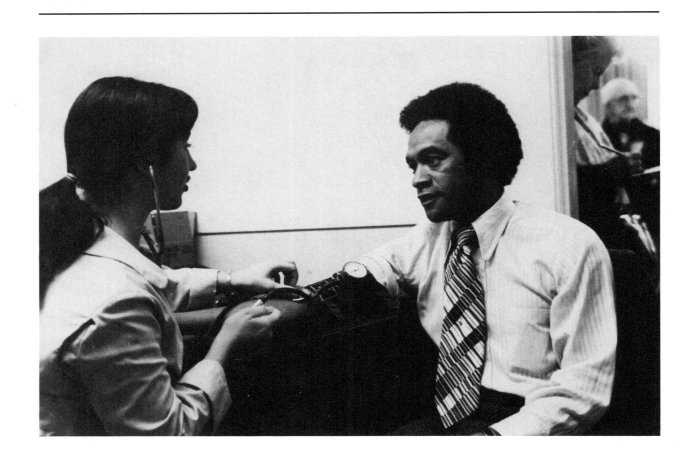

When do you see a doctor?

 Talk

healthy

sick

DISCUSSION

What do you do when you are sick?
Who takes care of sick people?
Why do people get sick?

MORE QUESTIONS

How do you take care of yourself?   Your family?
When do you take medicine?
Where do you buy medicine?
When do you see a doctor?
When do you need to make an appointment?
What do you do if you see someone hurt on the street?
Who takes care of people when they are sad or depressed?
What do you do if someone dies?

SUMMARY

How can you stay healthy?
How can your family stay healthy?

 # Write and Read

When? _____

What? _____

Where? _____

When? _____

What? _____

Where? _____

60

When? _____

What? _____

Where? _____

When? _____

What? _____

Where? _____

 Listen

1.	cap	lap	clap
2.	sip	lip	slip
3.	pan	lan	plan
4.	cock	lock	clock
5.	sot	lot	slot
6.	pot	lot	plot
7.	sed	led	sled
8.	pug	lug	plug
9.	cot	lot	clot
10.	sam	lam	slam
11.	pum	lum	plum
12.	cash	lash	clash

1.	pass	pat	past
2.	bess	bet	best
3.	lass	lat	last
4.	miss	mit	mist
5.	loss	lot	lost
6.	an	ad	and
7.	ben	bed	bend
8.	han	had	hand
9.	ban	bad	band
10.	win	wid	wind
11.	sit	sick	
12.	bat	back	
13.	chet	check	
14.	lot	lock	
15.	hat	hack	

Analyze

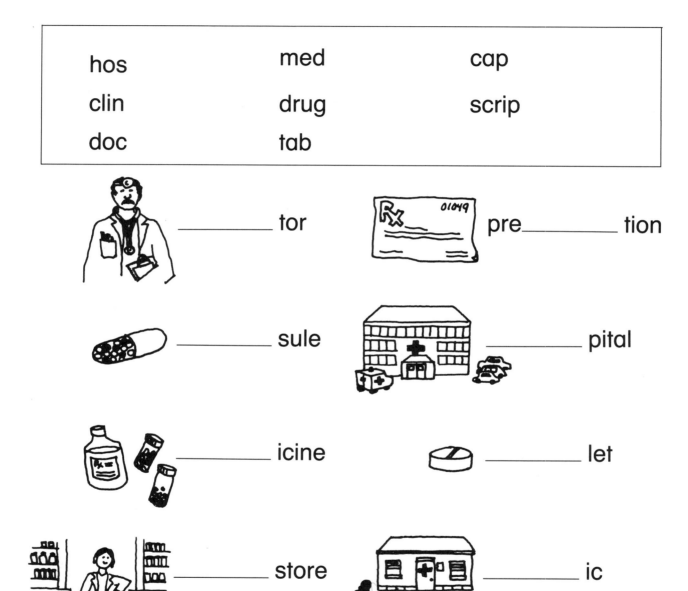

hos	med	cap
clin	drug	scrip
doc	tab	

_____ tor

pre_____ tion

_____ sule

_____ pital

_____ icine

_____ let

_____ store

_____ ic

 **Explain**

1. _____ leg hurts.

2. _____ neck hurts.

3. His chest _____ .

4. _____ back hurts.

5. Her head _____ .

 **Look**

A.

January 12	*Apr. 12*	*Jan. 12*
March 28	*Mar. 28*	*Nov. 28*
April 14	*Sept 14*	*Apr. 14*
October 5	*Dec 5*	*Oct. 5*
February 17	*Jul. 17*	*Feb. 17*
December 30	*Aug. 30*	*Dec. 30*
November 18	*Nov. 18*	*May 18*

B.

Monday	*Wed.*	*Mon.*	*Thurs.*
Friday	*Tues*	*Thurs.*	*Fri.*
Wednesday	*Wed.*	*Tues.*	*Mon.*
Tuesday	*Thurs.*	*Fri.*	*Tues.*
Thursday	*Tues.*	*Mon.*	*Thurs.*
Sunday	*Sat.*	*Sun.*	*Fri.*
Saturday	*Sun*	*Thurs.*	*Sat.*

C.

Friday, August 27	Fri. Aug. 27	Fri. Apr. 27
Tuesday, September 12	Tues. Aug 12	Tues. Sept. 12
Monday, November 20	Mon. Mar. 20	Mon. Nov. 20
Thursday, March 7	Thurs. May 7	Thurs. Mar. 7
Wednesday, February 10	Wed. Dec. 10	Wed. Feb. 10
Saturday, May 17	Sat. May 17	Sat. Nov. 17
Monday, July 18	Mon. Jul. 18	Mon. Jan 18
Friday, January 29	Fri. Jan. 29	Fri. Nov. 29
Monday, October 15	Tues. Oct. 15	Mon. Oct. 15
Tuesday, April 30	Thurs. Apr. 30	Tues Apr. 30
Wednesday, December 4	Wed. Dec. 4	Mon. Dec. 4
Sunday, September 5	Sun. Sept. 5	Sat. Sept. 5

Do

JAMES E. HARRISON, M.D.
290 Prospect St. Suite 104   Chicago, IL 60610

Pete Dallas
HAS AN APPOINTMENT ON

Wed.   _Oct._   _31_
DAY   MONTH   DATE

AT_____ A.M. _1:30_ P.M.

PLEASE TELEPHONE ONE DAY IN ADVANCE IF YOU WILL BE
UNABLE TO KEEP THE APPOINTMENT
PHONE: 893-5550.

What time?
Who?
What day?

JAMES E. HARRISON, M.D.
290 Prospect St. Suite 104   Chicago, IL 60610

Marie Kirkos
HAS AN APPOINTMENT ON

Mon.   _Jan._   _14_
DAY   MONTH   DATE

AT_9:45_ A.M. _____ P.M.

PLEASE TELEPHONE ONE DAY IN ADVANCE IF YOU WILL BE
UNABLE TO KEEP THE APPOINTMENT
PHONE: 893-5550.

What day?
What time?
Who?

JAMES E. HARRISON, M.D.
290 Prospect St. Suite 104   Chicago, IL 60610

Sonia Lake
HAS AN APPOINTMENT ON

Fri   _Apr._   _10_
DAY   MONTH   DATE

AT_11:00_ A.M. _____ P.M.

PLEASE TELEPHONE ONE DAY IN ADVANCE IF YOU WILL BE
UNABLE TO KEEP THE APPOINTMENT
PHONE: 893-5550.

Who?
What day?
What time?

JAMES E. HARRISON, M.D.
290 Prospect St. Suite 104   Chicago, IL 60610

Anthony Ponti

HAS AN APPOINTMENT ON

Tues.   *Feb.*   *24*

DAY   MONTH   DATE

AT_____ A.M. *2:30* P.M.

PLEASE TELEPHONE ONE DAY IN ADVANCE IF YOU WILL BE
UNABLE TO KEEP THE APPOINTMENT
PHONE: 893-5550.

Who? _____
What day? _____
What time? _____

JAMES E. HARRISON, M.D.
290 Prospect St. Suite 104   Chicago, IL 60610

Pam Gillis

HAS AN APPOINTMENT ON

Fri   *Nov.*   *8*

DAY   MONTH   DATE

AT *10:15* A.M. _____ P.M.

PLEASE TELEPHONE ONE DAY IN ADVANCE IF YOU WILL BE
UNABLE TO KEEP THE APPOINTMENT
PHONE: 893-5550.

What time? _____
Who? _____
What day? _____

JAMES E. HARRISON, M.D.
290 Prospect St. Suite 104   Chicago, IL 60610

Kirsten Keller

HAS AN APPOINTMENT ON

Wed.   *Sept.*   *29*

DAY   MONTH   DATE

AT *8:45* A.M. _____ P.M.

PLEASE TELEPHONE ONE DAY IN ADVANCE IF YOU WILL BE
UNABLE TO KEEP THE APPOINTMENT
PHONE: 893-5550.

What day? _____
What time? _____
Who? _____

JAMES E. HARRISON, M.D.
290 Prospect St. Suite 104   Chicago, IL 60610

Jim Ross

HAS AN APPOINTMENT ON

Thurs.   *Mar.*   *3*

DAY   MONTH   DATE

AT_____ A.M. *1:00* P.M.

PLEASE TELEPHONE ONE DAY IN ADVANCE IF YOU WILL BE
UNABLE TO KEEP THE APPOINTMENT
PHONE: 893-5550.

Who? _____
What time? _____
What day? _____

Do

LEVIN'S PHARMACY
No. 175—734   5/8/86
Martha Martinas
Take 1 capsule every six hours.
Knight

Who? _____
How many? _____
When? _____

BAY ST. DRUG STORE
No. 148435   9/4/85
David Prophete
Take 1 tsp. every three hours.
Foster

Who? _____
How much? _____
When? _____

HADLEY'S DRUGSTORE
No. 175582   12/5/86
Paul Jules
Take 1 tablet four times daily.
Fegley

Who? _____
How many? _____
When? _____

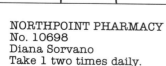

NORTHPOINT PHARMACY
No. 10698
Diana Sorvano
Take 1 two times daily.
Jezek

Who? _____
How many? _____
When? _____

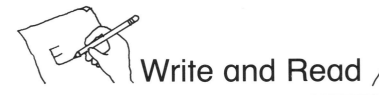 

_____

_____

_____

_____

_____

_____

_____

7
Landlords, Bugs, and Rent

How many people live here?

 **Talk**

```
┌─────────────────┐
│    housing      │
│    landlord     │
│     rent        │
└─────────────────┘
```

DISCUSSION

Where do you live now?
Where did you live in _____?
Who takes care of your housing?

MORE QUESTIONS

Do you pay rent?
Who is your landlord?
How many people live in your house or apartment?
Who are your neighbors?
Who fixes the sink?   Hall?   Windows?   Stove?   Ceiling?
Who cleans the hall?   Stairs?   Yard?
What can you do if there is no heat or hot water?
How long have you lived in _____?
How many times have you moved in the U.S.?
Where did you live before?
Will you move again?   Why or why not?
If the landlord raises the rent, what can you do?

SUMMARY

How can you get better housing?
What do you want to do about your housing?

Write and Read

Before   Now

Jean

Port-au-Prince
Haiti

$0/mo.

New Orleans, Louisiana

$225/mo.

(You)

Listen

1.	send	pend	spend
2.	sill	pill	spill
3.	sip	lip	slip
4.	sam	lam	slam
5.	sack	tack	stack
6.	sand	tand	stand
7.	sell	pell	spell
8.	sog	mog	smog
9.	sun	pun	spun
10.	sick	tick	stick
11.	sop	top	stop
12.	sell	mell	smell

Analyze

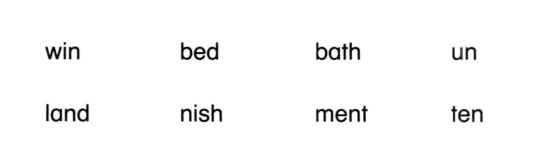

win	bed	bath	un
land	nish	ment	ten

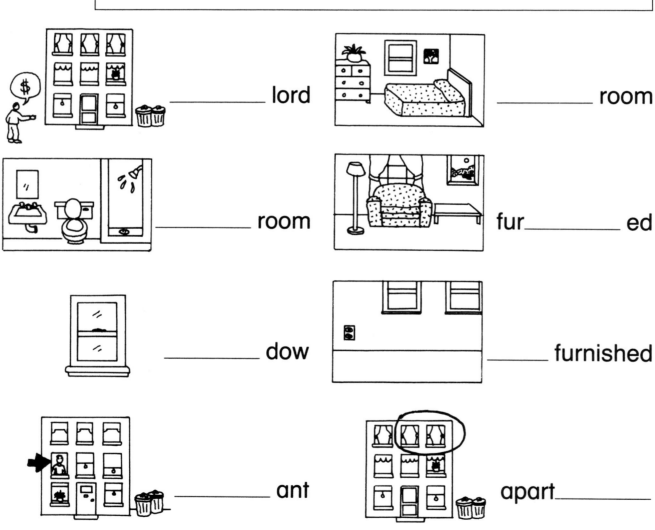

_____ lord

_____ room

_____ room

fur_____ ed

_____ dow

_____ furnished

_____ ant

apart_____

76

 Explain

telephone

bugs

call

rent

apartment

men

$250/mo.

Where do they live?

 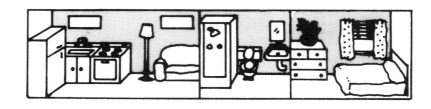

 Look

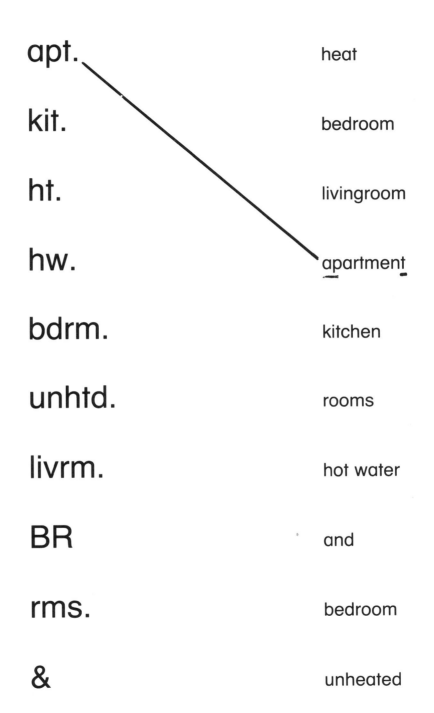

apt.	heat
kit.	bedroom
ht.	livingroom
hw.	apartment
bdrm.	kitchen
unhtd.	rooms
livrm.	hot water
BR	and
rms.	bedroom
&	unheated

 **Do**

FOR RENT

Belmont: Nr. Savin Hill.
Mod. 2 bdrm. apt.
ht.&hw., no pets, sec.,
ref. $425, 265-1187

What? _____

How much? _____

Where? _____

Rockaway: All new 2 lg.
BR, mod. kit., huge
livrm., dining area, no
ht., no pets, no fee,
$900 731-6634

What? _____

How much? _____

Where? _____

Valley Stream: Mod. htd.,
nice kit., 1 bdrm. $410
698-7575

What? _____

How much? _____

Where? _____

Westbury: 3 nice rms., nr.
school, $300 unhtd. No pets.
321-8740

What? _____

How much? _____

Where? _____

Sept. 1

Nov. 1

Jan. 1

_____

_____

_____

_____

_____

_____

 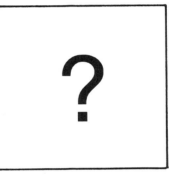

_____

_____

_____

_____

_____

_____

8
Money Matters

Why do people need money?

 Talk

> money
>
> welfare

DISCUSSION

What is welfare?

Who gets welfare?

Who took care of people in _____ ?

MORE QUESTIONS

Are you on welfare?

How do you get welfare?

How much money can you receive on welfare?

Does welfare pay for food? Rent? Clothing? Medicine?

How much money do you spend on rent? Food? Your children?

What bills must you pay?

Do you save any money? How can you save money?

Where do you buy food? Clothes? Medicine?

Do you ever spend too much money?

How long can you get welfare?

If you get a job, will you get welfare?

What pays for welfare?

What do Americans say about welfare?

Do you have enough money?

SUMMARY

What do Americans think about welfare?

Why do people need welfare?

$12

$32

$39

$25

$25

$30

$180

$270

$610

June 1

Gezai Tesfaye

-$3

June 30

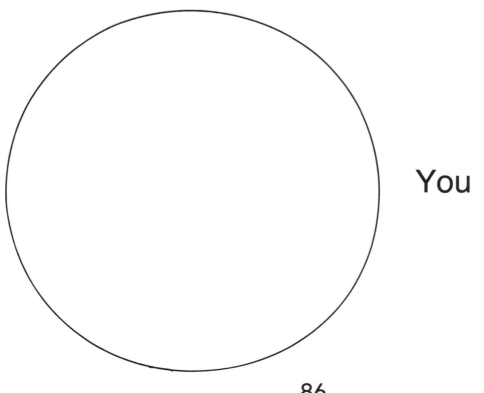

You

Listen

A.

1.	sam	same
2.	pan	pane
3.	dim	dime
4.	fin	fine
5.	rip	ripe
6.	cop	cope
7.	dat	date
8.	nam	name

B.

1.	h	at	ate	
2.	c	an	ane	
3.	t	ap	ape	
4.	b	it	ite	
5.	r	id	ide	
6.	n	ot	ote	
7.	t	im	ime	
8.	h	op	ope	

 Listen

1.  man
   mane

2. hat
   hate

3. *April 13, 1987* dat
   date

4.  pan
   pane

5.  dim
   dime

6.  at hom
   at home

7. *Mr. John Miller* nam
   name

8. fat
   fate

88

Analyze

in	lec	pen
tel	fif	dol
wel	bal	

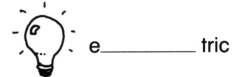 e_____ tric

 _____ lars

 _____ fare

 50 _____ ty

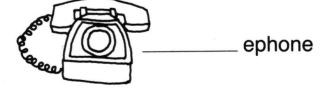 _____ ephone

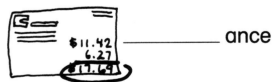 _____ ance

 ex_____ sive

 _____ come

$578/mo.

 **Explain**

month   week   day

1. We pay the telephone bill every _____ .

2. We pay the gas bill every _____ .

3. We pay the electric bill every _____ .

4. We pay the rent every _____ .

5. We pay the doctor every _____ .

6. We pay for the bus every _____ .

7. We pay for the food every _____ .

8. We pay for the medicine every _____ .

9. We pay for the clothes every _____ .

90

Look

Total   T A T O L G O T O T A L B A L T O T

Balance   E B C B L E N A B O L B A L A N C E

Amount   A N U O A M O U N T O A M E N T A O

Pay   P A P O Y A P E A P A Y N B A Y O P

AMOUNT	Number Account Amount Balance
PAY	Due Date Amount Due Discount Please Pay
TOTAL	Service Charge Total Due Estimated Bill State Tax
BALANCE	Readings Billing Date Beginning Date Balance Due

Do

Edison Electric Co.
P.O. Box 303
Pensacola, FL 32475

1.

Gezai Tesfaye
245 Market St.
Pensacola, FL 32478

Your Account Number   Service To
81-9254-0933   10 23 87

Please Pay $15.49
This Amount

Southern Telephone
P. O. Box 1
Fort Meyers, Florida 32456

2.

Gezai Tesfaye
245 Market Street
Pensacola, Florida 32478

ACCOUNT NUMBER   813 652-8834
BILL DATE: June 23, 1988
AMOUNT PAID

$.

TOTAL AMOUNT DUE
$ 14.37

Union Gas Co.
20 Prospect St.
Pensacola, FL 32475

PAYMENT DUE DATE   BALANCE DUE   ACCOUNT #   PAYMENT

12/22/87   32.40   603-951120 $.

3.

Gezai Tesfaye
245 Market St.
Pensacola, FL 32478
Customer Information
813 647-5145

Please Return This
with Your Payment.

Westwood Hospital   OUT-PATIENT STATEMENT
        DATE OF SERVICE
            2/15/88
BILL TO: _____
    R56999   R56999

4.

    Gezai Tesfaye   Tesfaye
    245 Market St.
    Pensacola, FL 32478 $78.65
                                          BALANCE DUE

First National Bank
Pensacola, Florida

Personal Money Order

3100746

$\frac{53-235}{113}$

_____ 19_____

Pay to the
order of _____

NOT VALID OVER $1,000.00

Amount 32 DOLS 40 CTS

Signature _____

Address _____

⑆074000065⑆ ⑈30994326⑈ 4994

First National Bank
Pensacola, Florida

Personal Money Order

3100747

$\frac{53-235}{113}$

_____ 19_____

Pay to the
order of _____

NOT VALID OVER $1,000.00

Amount 18 DOLS 49 CTS

Signature _____

Address _____

⑆074000065⑆ ⑈30994326⑈ 4994

First National Bank
Pensacola, Florida

Personal Money Order

3100748

$\frac{53-235}{113}$

_____ 19_____

Pay to the
order of _____

NOT VALID OVER $1,000.00

Amount 78 DOLS 65 CTS

Signature _____

Address _____

⑆074000065⑆ ⑈30994326⑈ 4994

First National Bank
Pensacola, Florida

Personal Money Order

3100749

$\frac{53-235}{113}$

_____ 19_____

Pay to the
order of _____

NOT VALID OVER $1,000.00

Amount 14 DOLS 37 CTS

Signature _____

Address _____

⑆074000065⑆ ⑈30994326⑈ 4994

93

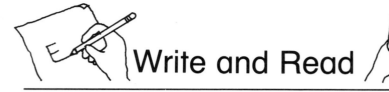 
	WANT	NEED

What do you think?

Adam Smith: People on Welfare don't need the money. They buy big cars, stereos and videos. Our taxes pay for Welfare. They don't want to work!

Irene de Silva: I need Welfare to pay for the rent, my children and food for my family. I can't find work.

9
Help! Help! Emergency!

What happened?

 Talk

emergency

help

DISCUSSION

What is an emergency?
Who helped with emergencies in _____ ?
Who can help you in the U.S.?

MORE QUESTIONS

When do you call for help?
What number do you call for help?
What do police do in the U.S.?
What did police do in _____ ?
Have you ever been robbed?   Where?   What happened?
Have you ever seen a fire?   Where?   What happened?
Have you ever had an accident?   Where?   What happened?
What do you say when you call 9 I I?
What do you tell children to do if they are lost?
How do you keep children safe?

SUMMARY

What can you do if there is an emergency?
How can you get help quickly?

 # Write and Read

Emergency	Who?	Phone #

 Listen

1. drill   frill   trill

2. trap   strap   wrap

3. crop   drop   trop

4. thrash   crash   trash

5. drip   trip   strip

6. crum   drum   strum

7. frog   grog   prog

8. crick   trick   brick

9. trunk   drunk   shrunk

10. brag   crag   drag

11. crit   grit   frit

12. shrug   frug   drug

Analyze

			+ ing
1.	hop	hope	
2.	run	rune	
3.	sit	site	
4.	rid	ride	
5.	shop	shope	
6.	rob	robe	
7.	stop	stope	
8.	writ	write	
9.	driv	drive	
10.	cut	cute	
11.	tak	take	
12.	rip	ripe	

 **Explain**

FIRE   POLICE   POISON

AMBULANCE   ACCIDENT   ALARM

POISON

ACCIDENT

1. _____

_____

2. _____

_____

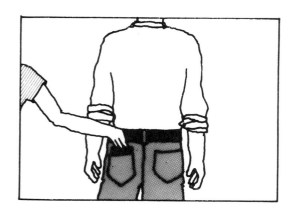

3. _____

_____

4. _____

_____

Damage

It is my car.

Witness

The car was hit in an accident.

Owner

I saw the accident.

Insurance

The men are hurt.

License

I passed a driving test.

Injured

They will help pay for the accident.

Registration

There is a form that shows it's my car.

 Look

1.	June 30, 1968	8/30/68	6/30/68	3/30/68
2.	March 21, 1967	3/21/67	2/21/67	12/21/67
3.	May 17, 1984	12/15/84	1/15/84	5/17/84
4.	August 9, 1978	8/9/78	9/9/78	4/9/78
5.	April 4, 1985	4/14/85	8/4/85	4/4/85
6.	July 14, 1981	8/14/81	7/14/81	7/4/81
7.	Feb. 12, 1985	2/12/85	12/12/85	3/12/85
8.	Nov. 20, 1980	7/20/90	11/20/80	12/20/80
9.	Sept. 7, 1987	9/7/87	7/7/87	8/7/87
10.	Jan. 3, 1970	3/3/70	6/3/70	1/3/70
11.	Oct. 29, 1952	8/29/52	10/29/82	10/29/52
12.	Dec. 19, 1963	19/12/63	2/19/63	12/19/63

 Do

ACCIDENT REPORT

Date of Accident	Day of the Week S M T W T F S ☐ ☐ ☐ ☐ ☐ ☐ ☐	A.M. ☐ P.M. ☐	Time

Name of Driver		Date of Birth	Sex ☐ ☐ M F

Address		Driver's License No.

Owner's Name and Address (if same, write "same")	Registration No.

Insurance Company	Car Year	Car Make	Car Type

Damage to Car

Name of Driver		Date of Birth	Sex ☐ ☐ M F

Address		Driver's License No.

Owner's Name and Address (if same, write "same")	Registration No.

Insurance Company	Car Year	Car Make	Car Type

Damage to Car

Witness	Address	Phone

Number Injured	Name of Hospital	Taken by Ambulance? ☐ Yes ☐ No

1.

2.

3.

4.

5.

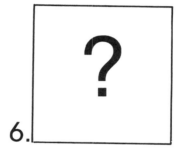

6.

_____

_____

_____

_____

_____

1.

2.

3.

4.

5.

6. ?

Many Colors, Many Dreams

10

What do Americans look like?

 **Talk**

immigrant
refugee
citizen

DISCUSSION

Why did you leave your country?
Why did you come to _____ ?
What can you and your family do in America?

MORE QUESTIONS

Why did you become a refugee or immigrant?
What is good about life in the U.S.?
What is bad about life here?
What do Americans look like?   Eat?   Wear?
What do you enjoy doing the most here?
What do you miss the most about your country?
Do you want to become a citizen?
What do you hope for your own future?
What do you hope for your family's future?

SUMMARY

What do you think about living in America?
What do you hope for as an American citizen?

 # Write and Read

	PAST (in _____)	PRESENT (in _____)	FUTURE (in ___?___)
happy			
sad			
angry			
scared			
bored			

Listen

A.

1. ____ e 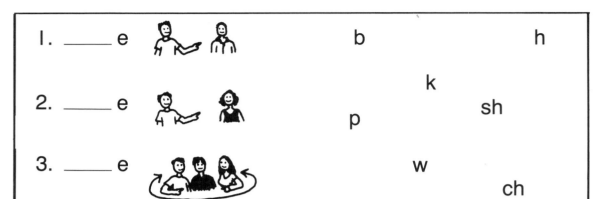   b   h

                                              k
2. ____ e   sh
                                   p

3. ____ e   w
                                                ch

B.

1. ____ ea ____ 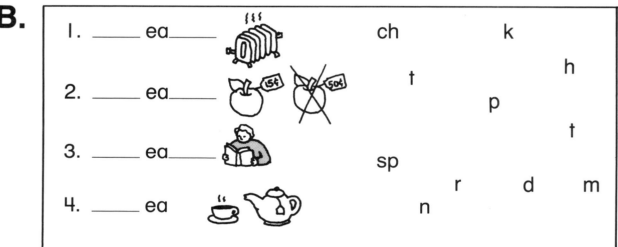   ch   k

                                                     h
2. ____ ea ____   t
                                         p

                                                    t
3. ____ ea ____   sp

                              r   d   m
4. ____ ea   n

C.

1. ____ ee ____    p   f

                                                       t
2. ____ ee ____   s   sw
                                    tr

3. ____ ee ____   w   n

                              k
4. ____ ee ____   m   d

112

D.

1. _____ ai _____   dr   r
                           n

2. _____ ai _____   p   l
                        t

3. _____ ai _____   s   tr   n

E.

1. _____ ay   gr
                     pl

2. _____ ay   d   st

                              p
3. _____ ay   n   b

F.

1. _____ oa _____   t
                          p   s

2. _____ oa _____   c
                          r   t

3. _____ oa _____   g
                    b   n   m

4. _____ oa _____   l   t
                              d

5. _____ oa _____   r   ch   d

 Explain

Why did you leave _____?

Why did you come to the U.S.?

Why do you live in _____?

Why do you go to school?

Why do you work so hard?

Why do you _____?

 # Explain

MONTH   January 10, (1980)

YEAR   September (5,) 1986

DAY   (August) 20, 1975

STREET   534 Glisan St.
                         Portland, (OR) 97220

ZIP CODE   534 Glisan St.
                         Portland, OR (97220)

CITY   534 (Glisan St.)
                         Portland, OR 97220

STATE   534 Glisan St.
                         (Portland,) OR 97220

 Look

Tel.	Month
St.	Year
Mo.	Street
Apt.	Telephone
Yr.	Apartment
Mos.	Number
Yrs.	Months
No.	Years

✓ sponsor	happy	street
refugees	excited	(month)
workers	scared	(day)
family	homesick	(year)
angry	hopes	(state)

THE DAILY   April 1, 1987

HAITIAN REFUGEES HOPE FOR A HAPPY FUTURE

The first Haitian family arrived in Bangor last week. Jean Paquin, a young father of three, is excited to be here but scared of the cold weather. Jean shared his story with the *Daily* last week in the family's new two-room apartment on Main Street.

Jean explained the family had to leave Haiti because an angry supervisor threatened to report him to the government for organizing other dock workers. Jean lost his job and could not find work. He contacted his brother in Boston who agreed to sponsor the family. When they arrived, they learned the brother had no work. Jean's brother suggested that the family move to find work.

"I chose Maine," Jean explained, "because I hope to get a job on the docks." So far he has no work but he hopes his experience will help. "When the warmer weather comes," he hopes, "I should be able to find work."

Asked if he misses Haiti, Jean replied, "Yes, we're homesick. We miss our family in Haiti and the warm weather."

 **Do**

| BIOGRAPHIC INFORMATION |

PLEASE PRINT OR TYPE

NAME _____ A-_____
   Last (Family)   First (Given)   Middle   Alien Registration #

COUNTRY OF BIRTH _____ _____
                                             Social Security #

NATIVE LANGUAGE _____ DATE OF BIRTH _____
                                                  Month Day Year

CURRENT ADDRESS _____
             # Street   Apt. #   City   State   Zip Code

TELEPHONE NUMBER (_____) _____

There are _____ people in my household. They are:

NAME	SEX M/F	DATE OF BIRTH mo/day/yr	COUNTRY OF BIRTH	ALIEN NUMBER	WORKING yes no	SCHOOL yes no
(self)					☐ ☐	☐ ☐
					☐ ☐	☐ ☐
					☐ ☐	☐ ☐
					☐ ☐	☐ ☐
					☐ ☐	☐ ☐

Signature _____ Date _____

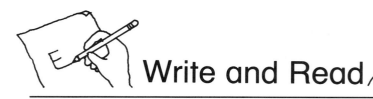 

1.

2.

3.

4.

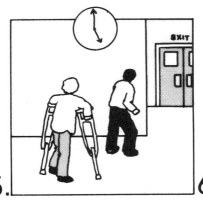

5.

6.

_____

_____

_____

_____

_____

_____

_____

Now write about your day.

11

Three to Eleven

Where can people find work?

 # Talk

workers

pay

benefits

DISCUSSION

Where can people find work?
What kind of work do they do?
What benefits can workers get?

MORE QUESTIONS

Do you work? What do you do?
What time do you work? Where?
What is your work like?
Is your work ever noisy, busy, dangerous, easy?
Have you ever been laid off?
Why do people get laid off?
How much is minimum wage?
How much do people in your work get paid?
How can you get more pay?
What do you want besides more pay?
Do you see women, Blacks, or immigrants at your workplace?
What jobs do minorities do?

SUMMARY

How can you get another or a better job?
How can you get better benefits?

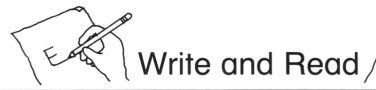 

Write and Read

Nina Mostello
Washington, D.C.

Job	housekeeper
Pay	$ 6.25 /hr.
Hours	from 3 p.m. to 11 pm
Skills	I can clean rooms
	change beds
	vacuum halls
	wash windows

Job	
Pay	$_____ /hr.
Hours	from _____ to _____
Skills	I can _____

Analyze

un- (not)	+	wrap tie plug pack

1. Please _____ in the TV.

2. Please _____ the TV.

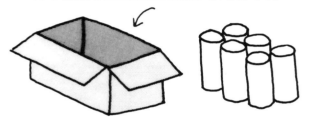

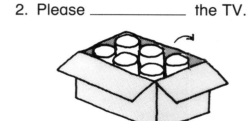

3. Please _____ the box.

4. Please _____ the box.

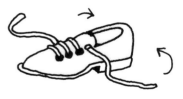

5. Please _____ the shoe.

6. Please _____ the shoe.

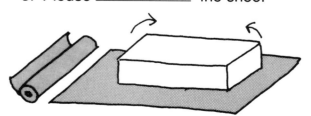

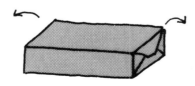

7. Please _____ the box.

8. Please _____ the box.

124

in- (not)	+	complete dependent expensive correct experienced valid

 $9,750

1. This car is _____ .

 $ 700

2. This car is _____ .

NAME Kim
ADDRESS 287 Green St.

TEL.# _____

3. The application is _____ .

NAME Kim Chen
ADDRESS 287 Green St.
Homer, LA 43972
TEL.# 891-6620

4. The application is _____ .

12 + 4 = 16

5. This problem is _____ .

12 + 4 = 18

6. This problem is _____ .

7. The baby is _____ on his mother.

8. The _____ man does not need help.

DRIVERS LICENSE
- OK -

9. My driver's license is still _____ .

DRIVERS LICENSE
Expires 6/84

10. Her driver's license is _____ .

WORK EXPERIENCE 5 YEARS

11. The _____ man has worked here for 5 years.

WORK EXPERIENCE 0

12. The _____ man has not had a job yet.

125

 # Explain

pay day	I get paid every week. Friday is _____ .	
hours	My working _____ are from three to eleven.	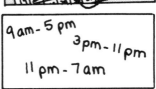
salary	Fourth of July, New Year's, and Christmas are _____ .	
insurance	My _____ is $350/week.	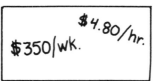
vacation	I stayed home with a fever. I took two days of _____ .	
holidays	When he broke his leg on the job, he got _____ .	
workmen's compensation	This job does not have health _____ .	
sick leave	Our company only gives two weeks _____ a year.	

 Look

exp.   hours

ben.   week

hrs.   benefits

ins.   experience

wk.   full time

mo.   necessary

yr.   month

f.t.   year

p.t.   temporary

nec.   insurance

temp.   part-time

sal.   salary

127

Do

1.

FACTORY HELP
Window assemblers needed. No exp. nec. P.T. 20 hrs/wk. See Bill at 339 Franklin St., Acton.

What? _____
Where? _____
When? _____
Who? _____

2.

MARRIOT FOOD SERVICE
Cashier/Line Server. Mon.-Fri. 6-2:00; 8 holidays, good starting sal., exp'd preferred. South Lincoln area. Call 973-3587.

What? _____
Where? _____
When? _____
Skills? _____
Who? _____

3.

CARPENTERS
Exp'd carpenters wanted for temp. work. Good pay, no ben. 6 days/wk. Call 774-2396.

What? _____
When? _____
Skills? _____
Benefits? _____
Who? _____

4.

DRIVERS & WIPERS
Start today. No exp. nec. F.T., good sal. Apply in person: CAR WASH, 314 Bacon St., Pembroke.

What? _____
Where? _____
When? _____
Skills? _____
Who? _____

5.

PRINTER
Min. 3 yrs. exp.; must operate A B Dick 360 machine. $6/hr. full ins. coverage. KELLY OFFSET, Medford 674-8200.

What? _____
Where? _____
Skills? _____
Pay? _____
Benefits? _____

 Do

APPLICATION FOR EMPLOYMENT

AN EQUAL OPPORTUNITY EMPLOYER M/F

NAME (LAST, FIRST, MIDDLE INITIAL) PLEASE PRINT	AREA CODE	PHONE NUMBER	SOCIAL SECURITY NUMBER

PRESENT ADDRESS (NO., STREET, CITY, STATE AND ZIP CODE)	U.S. CITIZEN □ YES □ NO

POSITION DESIRED	FULL TIME □	PART TIME □	TEMP. □	PAY EXPECTED	IF NO, ARE YOU A LAWFULLY IMMIGRATED RESIDENT ALIEN? □ YES □ NO

EMPLOYMENT RECORD	LAST OR PRESENT JOB	2	3
COMPANY NAME			
ADDRESS			
CITY & STATE			
JOB			
DATES OF EMPLOYMENT	FROM: / / TO: / /	FROM: / / TO: / /	FROM: / / TO: / /
WHOM MAY WE CONTACT?			
WHAT DID YOU DO? (USE EXTRA SHEET IF NECESSARY)		WHAT DID YOU DO? (USE EXTRA SHEET IF NECESSARY)	WHAT DID YOU DO? (USE EXTRA SHEET IF NECESSARY)
WHY DID YOU LEAVE? (OR, WHY ARE YOU LEAVING?)		WHY DID YOU LEAVE?	WHY DID YOU LEAVE?

Person to be notified in case of accident or emergency

NAME _____

ADDRESS _____ PHONE NUMBER_____

I certify that the facts on this Application are true and complete to the best of my knowledge.

DATE _____ SIGNATURE _____

129

1982

1987

_____

_____

_____

_____

_____

_____

_____

_____

_____

_____

_____

_____

_____

12
Family Ties

Is your family changing?

 Talk

family

DISCUSSION

How many people are in your family?
Where do your relatives live?
When do children become adults?
Who takes care of old people?

MORE QUESTIONS

Who lives in your house?
Where do mothers give birth?   Who helps when a baby is born?
What do children do at home?   Who do they play with?
Do children listen to adults?   What do you do if they don't?
Can children smoke?   Date?   Work?   Drink?   Marry?
How old must they be to do these things?
What must parents do for their children?
How do people decide to get married? Separated? Divorced?
When do people retire?
What do old people do?

SUMMARY

How are American families different from families in _____ ?
Is your family changing?

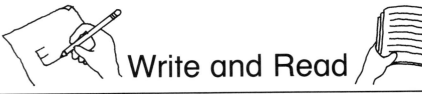

Write and Read

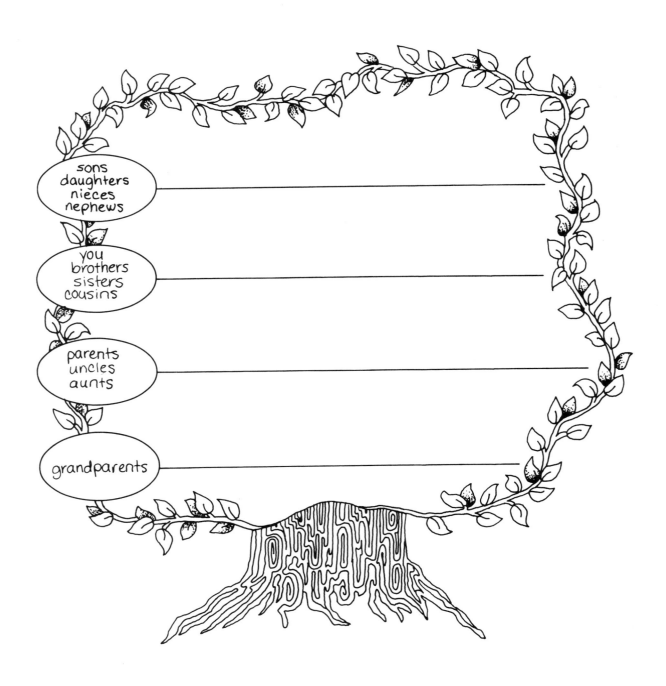

sons
daughters
nieces
nephews

you
brothers
sisters
cousins

parents
uncles
aunts

grandparents

 Listen

A.

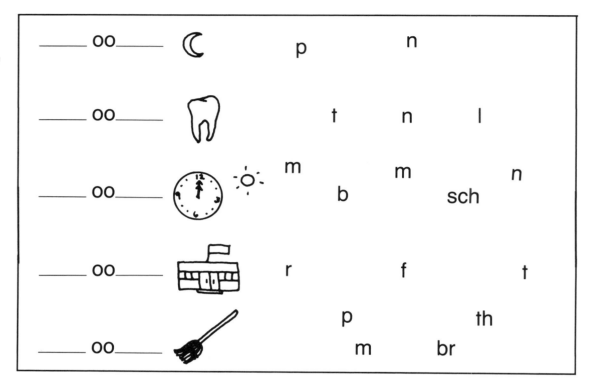

___ oo ___ 🌙	p	n
___ oo ___ 🦷	t	n	l
___ oo ___ 🕐 ☀️	m	m	n
	b	sch
___ oo ___ 🏫	r	f	t
___ oo ___ 🧹	p	th
	m	br

B.

___ aw	y	d
___ aw	l	t
	n	
___ aw ___	s	cr
	l	
___ aw ___	m	dr	p

C.

_____ au _____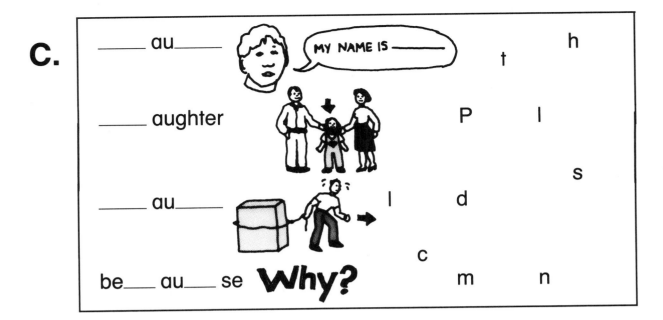

_____ aughter

_____ au _____

be ___ au ___ se **Why?**

h
t
P   l
s
l   d
c
m   n

D.

_____ igh _____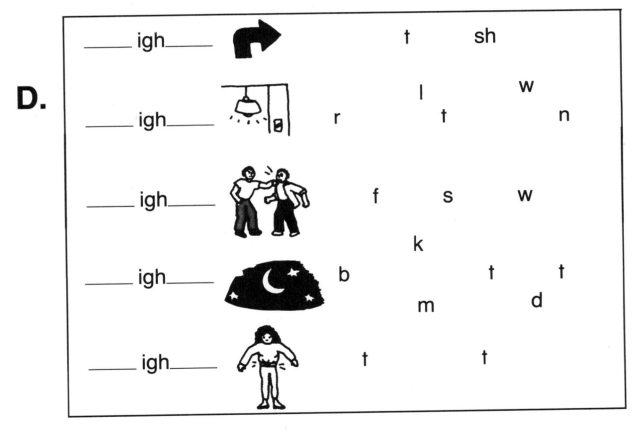

_____ igh _____

_____ igh _____

_____ igh _____

_____ igh _____

t   sh
l   w
r   t   n
f   s   w
k
b   t   t
m   d
t   t

137

 Explain

son

dependents

wife

daughter

husband

divorced

maiden name

widowed

married

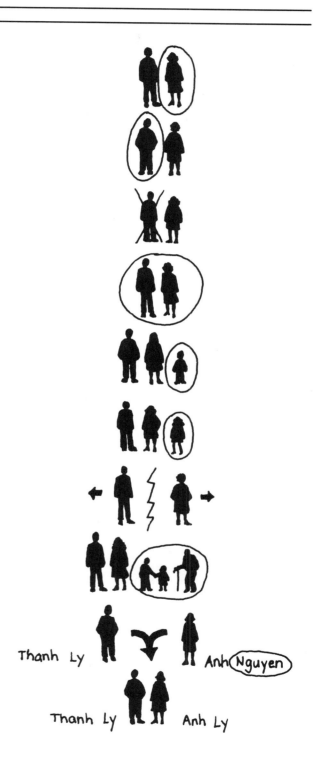

Thanh Ly   Anh Nguyen

Thanh Ly   Anh Ly

Explain

Categorize

neck   daughter   leg
happy   head   husband
son   sad   scared
address   back   nose
angry   name   parents
children   date   telephone #
birthplace   hand   age
chest   bored   wife

Feelings	Family	Body	Personal Information

 Look

Birthplace	(Maiden)	Age
Father	Widowed	Mother
Occupation	Marriage	Divorced

NOTICE OF INTENTION OF MARRIAGE

(PLEASE PRINT) ...September... 23 19 84

TO THE .... CLERK OF ...Cambridge... MASS.

SIR: The following notice of intention of marriage is hereby given in compliance with law.

GROOM	BRIDE
Present Name, Thanh Van Ly	Present Name, Anh Thi Nguyen
Surname to be used after marriage, Ly	Surname to be used after marriage, Ly
Age, 28	Age, 23
RESIDENCE:	RESIDENCE:
28 Inman St.	288 Harvard St.
(Street and Number)	(Street and Number)
Cambridge MA	Cambridge MA
(City or town) (State or country)	(City or town) (State or country)
Marriage, first, second, etc. First	Marriage, first, second, etc. First
(Widowed or divorced) —	(Widowed or divorced) —
Occupation, Cook	Occupation, Stitcher
BIRTHPLACE:	BIRTHPLACE:
Saigon Vietnam	Hue Vietnam
(City or town) (State or country)	(City or town) (State or country)
Father's name Tuan Xuan Ly	Father's name Hai Van Nguyen
Mother's name Chi Minh Nguy	Mother's name Cuc Thi Tran
(Given) (Maiden)	(Given) (Maiden)

Applicants { *Thanh Van Ly*
Anh Thi Nguyen

Subscribed and sworn to, before me, this .... day of .... A.D., 19......

140

 Do

STANDARD CERTIFICATE OF BIRTH

CHILD

NAME _____
     First   Middle   Last

SEX _____ DATE _____ HOUR _____
             OF   Month   Day   Year
             BIRTH

FATHER

NAME _____
     First   Middle   Last

BIRTHPLACE _____
           City or Town   State or Country

DATE _____
OF   Month   Day   Year
BIRTH

MOTHER

NAME _____
     First   Middle   Last

MAIDEN NAME _____

BIRTHPLACE _____
           City or Town   State or Country

DATE _____
OF   Month   Day   Year
BIRTH

ADDRESS _____
        No.   Street   City or Town   State   Zip Code

I certify that the information above is true
and correct.

_____
           (Signature)

_____
(Relationship)   (Date)

141

MEDICAL CLAIM FORM

COMMONWEALTH INSURANCE COMPANY

Please type or print

PART 1:	
EMPLOYEE'S NAME (Last) (First)	SOC. SEC. NO.
PATIENT'S NAME, IF CLAIM IS FOR DEPENDENT	
EMPLOYER	INSURANCE PLAN NO.
EMPLOYER'S ADDRESS (No., Street, City, State, Zip Code)	

PART 2:

THIS CLAIM IS FOR ☐ EMPLOYEE ☐ SPOUSE ☐ CHILD	DATE OF BIRTH OF THIS PERSON
NATURE OF ILLNESS OR INJURY	IF ACCIDENT, STATE WHEN, WHERE AND HOW IT HAPPENED
ARE YOU ☐ SINGLE ☐ MARRIED ☐ WIDOWED	☐ DIVORCED ☐ SEPARATED

IF YOU ARE MARRIED OR SEPARATED

NAME OF SPOUSE	SPOUSE'S SOC. SEC. NO.	IS YOUR SPOUSE EMPLOYED? ☐ YES ☐ NO

IF CLAIM IS FOR YOUR DEPENDENT OTHER THAN SPOUSE

NAME OF DEPENDENT	☐ SINGLE ☐ MARRIED ☐ DIVORCED ☐ SEPARATED

Signed (Employee) _____ Date _____

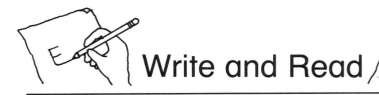 
Birth

?

?

?

_____

_____

_____

_____

Growing Up

_____

_____

_____

_____

_____

_____

Marriage

Death

Family Life

13
More Education?

Does education make a difference?

 **Talk**

```
education
training
teachers
```

DISCUSSION

Who goes to school in your family?
Why do people go to school?
How important was education in _____ ?

MORE QUESTIONS

What can you learn at school?
When can adults study?
Where can they study?
Do you need more education?
What education or training do you need for your work?
What education or training do you need to get a better job?
Does school cost money? How much?
How can you get loans or financial aid for your education?
What do people think about teachers?
What do Americans think about more degrees?
What do you think about your own education?
Who in your family should study?

SUMMARY

How can school help your family?
Does education make a difference?

Write and Read

The Life and Times of
Ines Chavez

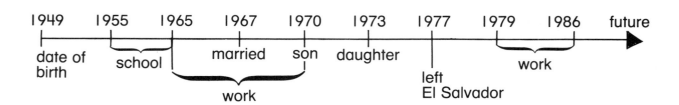

1949   1955   1965   1967   1970   1973   1977   1979   1986   future

date of   school   married   son   daughter   work
birth   work   left
                                                    El Salvador

 # Listen

A.

_____ ow _____	⬇	n		cr
_____ ower		p	d	t
_____ ow _____		n m	c	fl
_____ ow _____		s		n
_____ ow _____		b	d	

B.

_____ ou _____		r	s	nd
_____ ound		th	b	p
_____ ound	1 lb.	m	t	h
_____ ouse	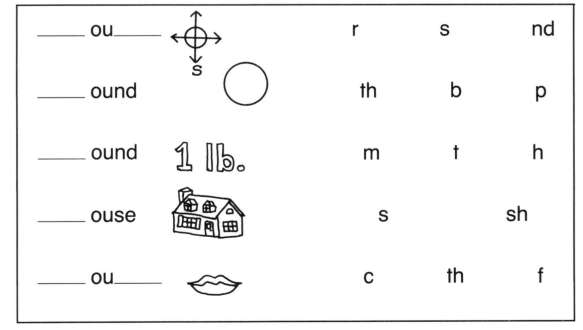	s		sh
_____ ou _____		c	th	f

Analyze

1.	a	ple	ble	tle
2.	ap	ple	ble	tle
3.	ta	ple	ble	tle
4.	sim	ple	ble	tle
5.	lit	ple	ble	tle
6.	tem	ple	ble	tle
7.	sam	ple	ble	tle
8.	exam	ple	ble	tle
9.	bot	ple	ble	tle
10.	ti	ple	ble	tle
11.	peo	ple	ble	tle
12.	tri	ple	ble	tle

152

 Explain

elementary school	Teenagers study at _____ .	13-18 years old
bilingual	After high school, they can study at a _____ .	18⁺ years old
community college	Young children study at _____ school.	6-12 years old
vocational	Before, he didn't finish high school. Later he studied and got his _____ .	
G.E.D.	They are studying to be cooks at _____ school.	½ CUP
high school	Some children study both in Spanish and in English. They are in a _____ program.	Spanish/English English/Chinese
adult education	He finished high school. Now he has a _____ .	
diploma	The school tells students if they are doing well or poorly in class. The school gives _____ .	ENGLISH A MATH C⁺ SCIENCE B
grades	_____ has classes at night for ESL, GED, and other training.	18⁺ years old

 # Look

---

adult	study	graduates
register	vocational	English
training	GED	education
financial aid	high school	fees

COMMUNITY EDUCATION CENTER

The Community Education Center offers adult education classes.
The center is open from 6:30 p.m. to 9:30 p.m. Monday through
Friday. The programs offered are:

High School Equivalency (GED)

Adult Basic Education (ABE)

English as a Second Language (ESL)

Classes are held at 807 River Street. Some graduates of our programs
have entered community colleges and vocational training.

You may register Mondays between 6:30 and 9:30 p.m. Fees for
the programs are based on a sliding scale. Some financial aid is available.

Do

APPLICATION FOR ADMISSION

South State Community College
Office of Admissions
990 Hinckley Road
Houston, Texas 77084

A $10 Application Fee must accompany this application. Make checks payable to South State Community College. Answer all questions by printing or typing.

Last Name . . . .

First Name   Middle . . . .

Street Address . . . .

City . . . .

State, Zip Code . . . .

                                                           State   *Zip Code*

Home Telephone Number . . . .

                                                 Area Code   *Telephone Number*

Business Telephone Number . . . .

                                                 Area Code   *Telephone Number*

Social Security Number . . . .

Birthdate . . . .

                                                 Month   *Day*   *Year*

Sex   M(Male)   F(Female) . . . .

United States Citizen   Y(Yes)   N(No) . . . .

International Students   S(Student Visa), T(Temporary Visitor's Visa), P(Permanent Resident Alien), N(Not Applicable) . . . .

Check choice of Day or Evening and Entrance Date:

         ☐ Day   ☐ Evening

         ☐ Fall Semester 19__   ☐ Spring Semester 19__

         ☐ Summer Session 19__

(over)

Previous Education:

☐ grades 1–8   ☐ high school diploma

☐ some high school   ☐ technical school certificate

☐ technical school   ☐ GED

Type of School	Check if Still Attending	Check if Completed
☐ High School	☐	☐
☐ Technical/Vocational	☐	☐
☐ Other _____	☐	☐

English Language Proficiency:

☐ None   ☐ Fair   ☐ Excellent

☐ A few words   ☐ Good

Other Languages: (1—Poor, 2—Fair, 3—Good, 4—Excellent)

	Oral	Written

I certify that the foregoing statements on this application are true, complete, and accurate.

Signature _____ Date _____

156

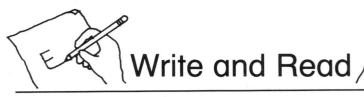 

157

Dealing with Discrimination

14

What is discrimination?

 Talk

| race |
| color |
| ethnic group |
| discrimination |

DISCUSSION

What makes people different?
Are there different kinds of people in your neighborhood?
How can different kinds of people live and work peacefully together?

MORE QUESTIONS

Which ethnic groups live in your neighborhood or work with you?
Which languages do your neighbors or co-workers speak?
Do people of different color live in your neighborhood or work with you?
Who do people discriminate against?
Why do people discriminate against others?
Has anyone ever discriminated against you?   What happened?
When should you report discrimination to the police or a social worker?

SUMMARY

What is discrimination?
When someone discriminates against you, what can you do?

Write and Read

Identity of Sophal Som

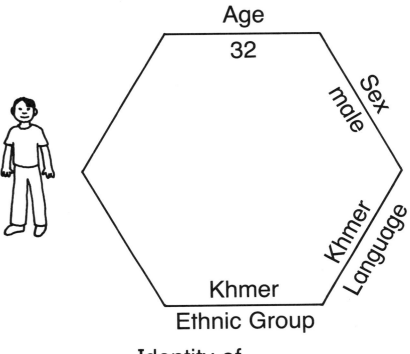

Age
32

Sex
male

Khmer
Language

Khmer
Ethnic Group

Identity of _____

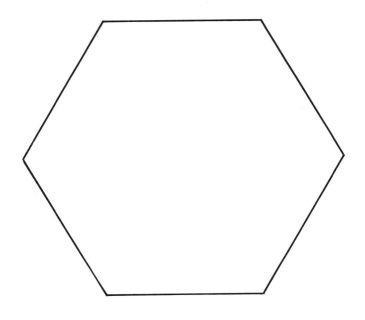

 Listen

A.

_____ ar _____ 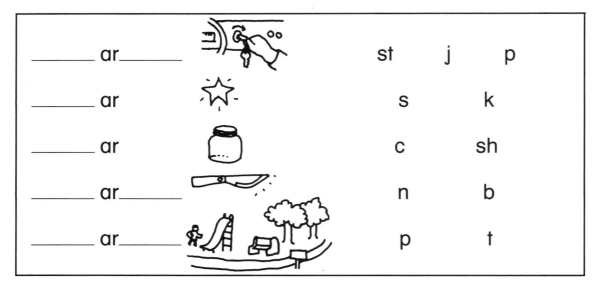 st   j   p

_____ ar   s   k

_____ ar   c   sh

_____ ar _____   n   b

_____ ar   p   t

B.

_____ ir _____ 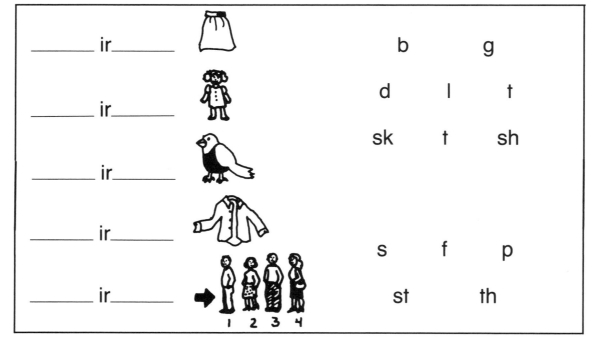 b   g

_____ ir _____   d   l   t

_____ ir _____   sk   t   sh

_____ ir _____   s   f   p

_____ ir _____   st   th

 Explain

Problem

Solution

Equal Pay Act of 1963
(Equal pay for equal work)

Age Discrimination in
Employment Act of 1967

Rehabilitation Act of
1973
(For the handicapped)

Civil Rights Act of
1964—Title VII
(For persons of color)

1978 Amendments to
Civil Rights Act
(Pregnant women are treated
the same as other workers)

163

Look

attack   problems   accuse   damages

prison   racial   threats

Community Responds to Racial Incident

Two white teenagers were charged in a racial attack against the Johnsons, a black family who recently moved into Charlestown. The teens are accused of threatening Peter, the family's seven year old son, and of dumping beer cans on their property.

Judge Gere ordered Mark Spencer and Bud Wilson to pay $500 in damages and to do five months of community service. He warned them that they would get up to three years in prison if they continued their threats.

Neighbors have rallied to the Johnson's support and are organizing a community action group to look into neighborhood problems. When asked how she felt about their efforts, Mrs. Johnson replied, "When those boys attacked my son we wanted to move but maybe we'll stay awhile longer."

 Look

---

| discrimination | sex | race | color | religion |
| national origin | equal | law | opportunity | |

Equal Employment Opportunity is...
THE LAW

**Private Employment,
State and Local Government,
Educational Institutions**

Race, Color, Religion, Sex, National Origin
Title VII of the Civil Rights Act of 1964, as amended, prohibits discrimination in hiring promotion, discharge, pay, benefits, etc. because of race, color, religion, sex or national origin.

Age
The Age Discrimination in Employment Act of 1967, as amended, prohibits age discrimination and protects applicants and employees aged 40–70 from discrimination in hiring, promotion, discharge, pay, benefits, etc.

Sex (wages)
The Equal Pay Act of 1963 as amended, prohibits sex discrimination in payment of wages to women and men doing equal work in the same workplace.

If you believe someone has discriminated against you, contact:

The U.S. Equal Employment Opportunity Commission
2410 "E" Street, N.W.
Washington, D.C. 20506
or telephone the EEOC District Office in your area.

Don't Forget...
Equal Employment Opportunity is the Law!

 **Do**

San Francisco Police Department

ICSS - Rm. 475, Hall of Justice
850 Bryant Street
San Francisco, CA 94103

Dear Citizen,

When this form is completed, it will serve as a San Francisco Police Incident Report which will document the occurrence and assist in its investigation. If you desire an incident report number, please call 553-1288 after five (5) business days.

FOR POLICE USE ONLY	CRIME CLASSIFICATION	ASSIGNED TO

PLEASE PRINT OR TYPE THE BELOW INFORMATION

GIVE ADDRESS OR LOCATION WHERE INCIDENT OCCURRED

DAY OF INCIDENT	DATE OF INCIDENT MO DAY YEAR	TIME	AM☐ PM☐	HOW ENTRY WAS MADE OR HOW DAMAGE OCCURRED

LAST NAME	FIRST NAME	MIDDLE NAME	RACE	SEX	DATE OF BIRTH MO DAY YEAR

RESIDENCE ADDRESS	CITY	ZIP	STATE	RES. PHONE AREA NUMBER

BUSINESS ADDRESS OR SCHOOL ATTENDED	CITY	ZIP	STATE	BUS. PHONE AREA NUMBER

DO YOU KNOW WHO IS RESPONSIBLE FOR THIS THEFT OR DAMAGE?   NAME   ADDRESS / SCHOOL

☐ YES   ☐ NO   IF YES, PLEASE DESCRIBE:

RACE   SEX   AGE   PHYSICAL DESCRIPTION

METHOD, TOOL, INSTRUMENT OR WEAPON USED	IF VEHICLE IS INVOLVED, DESCRIBE: YEAR MAKE MODEL
	☐ SUSPECT'S VEHICLE ☐ VICTIM'S VEHICLE
Give a brief summary of the incident below:	VEHICLE COLOR LICENSE NUMBER STATE

DESCRIBE WHAT WAS ☐ STOLEN ☐ LOST ☐ DAMAGED

ARTICLE	HOW MANY	MODEL/MODEL NO.	SERIAL NO.	CALIBER	COLOR	$VALUE
1.						
2.						
3.						
4.						
5.						

IT IS A MISDEMEANOR TO MAKE A FALSE REPORT OF A CRIME (SEC. 148.5 CALIF. PENAL CODE)

MO.   DAY   YEAR

DATE: _____

PLEASE SIGN YOUR NAME HERE

SFPD 28 (12/82)

Problem   Solution

_____

_____

_____

_____

_____

_____

Problem

Solution

_____

_____

_____

Problem

Solution

_____

_____

_____

15

Settling In

How long will you stay here?

 **Talk**

neighborhood

politicians

community

DISCUSSION

Who lives in your neighborhood?

What do you like about your neighborhood?

Who are the politicians in your community?

MORE QUESTIONS

Where do you like to go in your neighborhood?

Where does your family go out?

What does your family like to do in your neighborhood?

Why do you live in this neighborhood?

How long will you stay here?

What community organizations have you joined?

Who are the leaders of your community?   State?   Country?

How can politicians hear your concerns?

How can they help you?

Can you vote? Do you vote?

SUMMARY

How would you describe your neighborhood to a newcomer?

Who can help with problems in your neighborhood or community?

Write and Read

	Who?	Telephone #	Why?
neighbor			
school			
work			
health clinic			
police			
fire department			
child care			

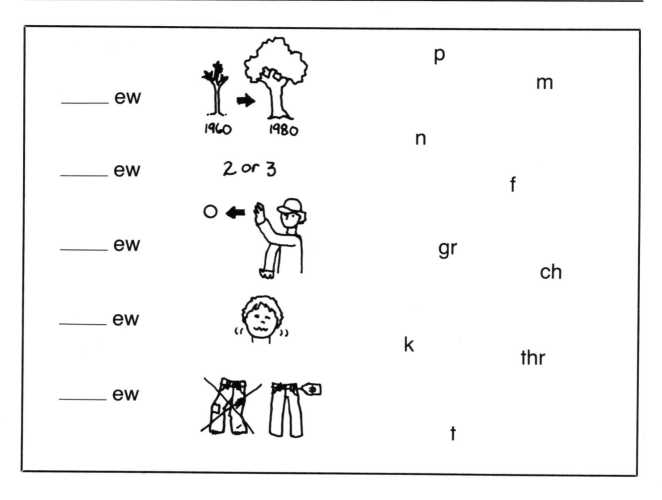

_____ ew

_____ ew   2 or 3

_____ ew

_____ ew

_____ ew

p

m

n

f

gr

ch

k

thr

t

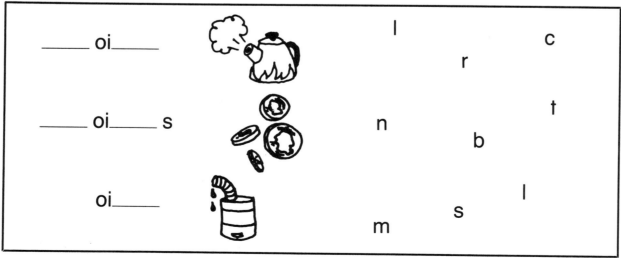

_____ oi_____

_____ oi_____ s

oi_____

l

c

r

t

n

b

m

s

l

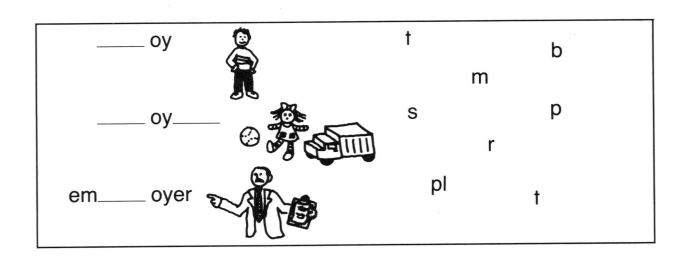

_____ oy   t   b

                         m

_____ oy _____   s   p

                     r

em _____ oyer   pl   t

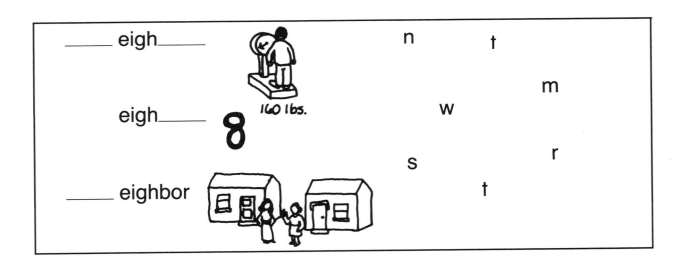

_____ eigh _____   n   t

                         m

eigh _____   w

                s   r

_____ eighbor   t

160 lbs.

8

 Explain

President	Local (City)
Governor	Federal (United States)
Mayor	State

President _____

Governor _____

Mayor _____

Senator _____

Senator _____

Congressman _____ in District _____

State Senator _____

State Senator _____

State Representative _____ in District _____

Look

Circle the phone number to call for a problem with:

1. landlord and apartment
2. green cards
3. driver's license
4. bus schedule
5. job discrimination

6. birth certificates
7. stolen car
8. housing discrimination
9. welfare information
10. sales tax

Government Listing Section

ALIEN INFORMATION - - - - - - - - - - - - 223-0201
  Tax Clearance Forms - - - - - - - - - - - - 523-1040
  Work Permits-Green Card - - - - - - - - - 223-2361
AUTOMOBILES
  Complaints-Attorney General - - - - - - - 727-8400
  Insurance Division - - - - - - - - - - - - - - 727-3333
  Merit Rating Board - - - - - - - - - - - - - - 727-7017
  Parking Violations - - - - - - - - - - - - - - 725-4131
  Registry Of Motor Vehicles - - - - - - - - 727-3723
  Stolen Vehicles-Boston - - - - - - - - - - 247-4535
BIRTH CERTIFICATES - - - - - - - - - - - 727-2840
BOARD OF HEALTH-BOSTON - - - - - - 725-4787
BUS SERVICE-MBTA - - - - - - - - - - - - 722-5657
  7 AM To 6 PM
    Mon To Fri - - - - - - - - - - - - - - - - 722-3200
  Nights & Wknds - - - - - - - - - - - - - - - 722-5000
CHILDREN & FAMILY SERVICES
  Child Abuse Inq-Federal - - - - - - - - - - 223-6450
  Welfare Assist - - - - - - - - - - - - - - - - 227-8320
CITY HALL
  Boston - 725-4000
CONGRESSIONAL OFFICES
  Area Info-FIC - - - - - - - - - - - - - - - - 223-7121
  US Senators
    Edward M Kennedy - - - - - - - - - - 223-2826
    Paul E Tsongas - - - - - - - - - - - - - 223-1890
DISCRIMINATION
  Employment
    Federal - - - - - - - - - - - - - - - - - - 223-4535
    State - 727-3990
  Housing - - - - - - - - - - - - - - - - - - - 223-4317
  Wage
    Federal - - - - - - - - - - - - - - - - - - 223-5272
    State - 727-3460
    Non-Payment - - - - - - - - - - - - - - 727-3464
EMERGENCY CALLS
  Boston - 911
  MDC Police - - - - - - - - - - - - - - - - - 523-1212
EMPLOYMENT SECURITY
  Boston - 727-6560
FIRE
  Boston - 911
FOOD STAMP INFO - - - - - - - - - - - - 727-6123
GARBAGE & TRASH
  COLLECTION-BOSTON - - - - - - - - 482-5300
GOVERNOR'S OFFICE INFO - - - - - - - 727-3600
HEALTH SERVICES
  Alcohol Drug Abuse & Mental Health

Info - 223-6827
Child Nutrition - - - - - - - - - - - - - - - - 223-6450
Disease Control Info - - - - - - - - - - - - 223-4045
Family Planning - - - - - - - - - - - - - - - 223-1673
Foreign Travel Immunizations - - - - - - 726-3570
Lead Poisoning - - - - - - - - - - - - - - - - 424-5965
Long Term Care Unit - - - - - - - - - - - - 223-6804
Maternal & Infant Care Info - - - - - - - - 223-1673
Public Health Service Hospital - - - - - - 782-3400
HOSPITALS
  See White Pages For Complete Listings
  Beth Israel - - - - - - - - - - - - - - - - - - 735-2000
  Boston City - - - - - - - - - - - - - - - - - 424-5000
  Brigham & Women's - - - - - - - - - - - - 732-5500
HOUSING
  Boston Bldg Problems & Complaints - - - 725-4787
  Discrimination Complaints - - - - - - - - - 223-4317
  Evictions-Legal Aid - - - - - - - - - - - - - 367-2880
HOUSING AUTHORITY
  Main Office 52 Chauncy Bos - - - - - - - 451-1250
    Central Maintenance Dept
      10 Kemp S Bos - - - - - - - - - - - 288-7951
    Central Stores 125 Amory Jam - - - - - 522-0700
IMMIGRATION &
NATURALIZATION
  INFORMATION - - - - - - - - - - - - - 223-0201
LEGAL SERVICES
  Housing Evictions - - - - - - - - - - - - - 367-2880
  Low Income Legal Aid - - - - - - - - - - - 367-2880
  Marital & Children's Legal Aid - - - - - - 227-0200
LICENSES
  Auto - 727-3723
  Business - - - - - - - - - - - - - - - - - - - 727-7030
  Driver - 727-3723
  Federal Firearms Licenses - - - - - - - - 223-7022
  Hunting & Fishing - - - - - - - - - - - - - 727-3153
  Learner's Permits - - - - - - - - - - - - - 727-3723
  Liquor - 727-3040
  Marriage-Boston - - - - - - - - - - - - - - 725-4000
  All Other Licenses - - - - - - - - - - - - - 727-7030
MEDICAID INQUIRIES - - - - - - - - - - - 227-8320
POISON CONTROL CENTER - - - - - - - 232-2120
POLICE DEPT
  Emergency Only - - - - - - - - - - - - - - - 911
  To Report Stolen Cars - - - - - - - - - - - 247-4535
  For All Other Business
    154 Berkeley Bos - - - - - - - - - - - 247-4200

COMMISSIONER'S OFFICE - - - - - - - - 247-4500
POLLUTION COMPLAINTS - - - - - - - - 223-7223
POST OFFICE
  General Info - - - - - - - - - - - - - - - - - 223-2451
PUBLIC ASSISTANCE &
WELFARE
  State - 727-6000
PUBLIC WORKS DEPT
  1 CITY HALL SQ BOS
  General Inf - - - - - - - - - - - - - - - - - 482-5300
  ADMINISTRATIVE OFCS
    Central Maintenance - - - - - - - - - - 482-5300
    Central Ofc Contracts - - - - - - - - - - 725-4912
    Highway Div
      Administrative Ofcs - - - - - - - - - 725-4949
      Maintenance Section - - - - - - - - 725-4950
      Sidewalks - - - - - - - - - - - - - - 725-4950
      Complaints - - - - - - - - - - - - - - 725-4947
      Street Lighting - - - - - - - - - - - - 482-5300
REGISTRY DIV
  1 CITY HALL SQ BOS
  Administrative Sec - - - - - - - - - - - - - 725-4175
  Birth Certificates - - - - - - - - - - - - - - 725-4177
  Death Certificates - - - - - - - - - - - - - 725-4184
  Marriage Certificates - - - - - - - - - - - 725-4179
  Registry Of Deeds - - - - - - - - - - - - - 725-8575
SOCIAL SECURITY INFO - - - - - - - - - 227-2400
TAXES
  City-Boston
    Excise Tax Info - - - - - - - - - - - - - 725-4122
    Real Estate - - - - - - - - - - - - - - - 725-4120
    Sewer - - - - - - - - - - - - - - - - - - 426-6046
  Federal
    Income - - - - - - - - - - - - - - - - - - 523-1040
    Forms - - - - - - - - - - - - - - - - - - 367-1040
    Inheritance Tax - - - - - - - - - - - - - 523-1040
  State
    Income - - - - - - - - - - - - - - - - - - 727-4545
    Sales - - - - - - - - - - - - - - - - - - - 727-4620
    Taxpayers Assist - - - - - - - - - - - - 727-4545
WELFARE INFO
  State - 727-6000
  Boston Office - - - - - - - - - - - - - - - - 227-8320
WORKMENS COMPENSATION
INFO
  Federal - - - - - - - - - - - - - - - - - - - 223-1815
  State - 727-3407

Do

Draw a map of your neighborhood. Write in places such as park, school, bus stop, police station, supermarket, drugstore, etc.

If you were mayor, what would you do?

I would _____

_____

_____

I would _____

_____

_____

_____

_____

_____

_____

_____

_____

_____

_____

Describe your own problem.

But I have a dream that . . .

Word List

Numbers refer to chapter numbers.

sales   15
Sat.   6
Saturday   6
scared   10
schedule   15
school   3
semester   13
Senator   15
separated   12
Sept.   6
September   6
sex   10
she   4
sick   6
sick leave   11
signature   5
single   12
skills   11
smoke   5
Soc. Sec. #   4
solution   14
son   12
speak   5
sponsor   10
spouse   12
spring   13
St.   10
state   10
stolen   15
street   10
study   13
summary   14
summer   13
Sun.   6
Sunday   6

t

tax   15
teachers   13

tel.   10
telephone   2
temp.   11
temporary   11
the   3
their   3
threat   14
three   6
Thurs.   6
Thursday   6
time   6
to   4
total   8
training   13
Tues.   6
Tuesday   6
two   6
type   9

u

unhtd.   7
U.S.A.   2

v

vacation   11
vocational   13

w

want   8
was   4
we   8
Wed.   6
Wednesday   6
week   8
welfare   8

184

what 4
when 4
where 4
who 6
why 10
widowed 12
wife 12
witness 9
wk. 11
women 2
work 4
workers 11
workmen's compensation 11
write 1

y

year 9
you 2

yr. 10
yrs. 10

z

zip code 10

Punctuation

. 2
? 2
4
$ 4
: 4
- 4
/ 4
' 5

Skills Index

PHONICS (Listen)

letter names, sounds	3–5, 7
short vowels, final	
consonants (v–c)	19, 28
consonant digraphs	39, 40
consonant-vowel-consonant	
(c-v-c)	39, 40, 49, 50
initial blends	62, 75, 99
final blends	63
long vowels (c-v-c-e) silent *e*	87, 88, 100
–ing	100
vowel digraphs	112, 113, 136, 137
–igh–	137
dipthongs	151, 172, 173
–eigh–	173
r–controlled vowels	162

STRUCTURAL ANALYSIS SKILLS (Analyze)

syllables	51, 64, 76, 89, 124, 125, 152
prefixes: negation	124, 125

COMPREHENSION SKILLS (Explain)

sound-symbol correspondence	9, 10
identification number	10
word level	20, 29, 30, 42, 101, 115, 138
sentence level	41, 52, 65, 103, 114
inferences	52, 53, 78
details	29, 30, 65, 90, 153
sequencing	77
main idea	102, 126
categorizing	139
analyzing	163
background knowledge	174

SIGHT WORD SKILLS (Look)

upper/lower case equivalents	11, 12
personal information	21, 31, 32, 54, 117
job information	122, 123, 128, 129
telling time	43
dates	
long form	22, 23
abbreviations	66, 67
numerical form	104
abbreviations	79, 116, 127
bill information	91
alphabetizing	175
household information	140
education information	154
legal information	164, 165

USABLE APPLICATIONS (Do)

reading signs	13, 14, 56
filling out forms	
simple applications	22, 23
school information	33
simple job applications	44
personal information	55
accident reports	105
biographic information	118
job applications	129
birth certificate worksheet	141
medical claim form	142
school applications	155, 156
police report form	166
reading appointment slips	68, 69
reading prescription labels	70
reading housing ads	80
reading bills	92
filling out money orders	93
reading job want ads	128
making a neighborhood map	176

LITERATE EXPRESSION (Write and Read Again)

creating a picture dictionary	15
writing captions	
(controlled writing)	24, 34, 35, 57
recording work histories	45
recording messages	71
describing problems	81–83
expressing an opinion	94, 95, 177–179
describing a situation	106–108
recording daily schedules	119, 120
reporting work situations	130–132
recording family histories	143–147
planning your future	157, 158
defending your position	167, 168

KEY WORDS (Write and Read)

literacy, read, write	1, 2
men, women	16–18
children, school, home	25–27
work experience	36–38
language, country	46–48
healthy, sick	58–61
housing, landlord, rent	72–74
money, welfare	84–86
emergency, help	96–98
immigrant, refugee, citizen	109–111
workers, pay, benefits	121–123
family	133–135
education, training, teachers	148–150
color, ethnic groups,	
discrimination	159–161
neighborhood, politicians,	
community	169–171